Perranaworthal Church

THE OLD
PARISH CHURCHES
OF CORNWALL

Mike Salter

FOLLY PUBLICATIONS

ACKNOWLEDGEMENTS

The photographs in this book were taken by the author between 1978 and 1998. He also prepared the map and the plans. The old prints, postcards and brass rubbings are reproduced from originals in his collection. Thanks to Andrea Kirkby for help with transport on one field trip in 1998, and to Marjorie Salter who checked the proofs.

ABOUT THIS BOOK

As with the other books about churches in this series (see the full list on the inside of the back cover) this book concentrates on the period before the Industrial Revolution of the late 18th century necessitated the construction of a fresh series of churches to serve the new urban areas. Most furnishings and monuments after 1790 are not mentioned but additions and alterations to older churches usually are, but with less detail. Churches founded after 1790 are not mentioned in the gazetteer, nor do they appear on the map. They are however listed towards the back of the book.

The book is inevitably very much a catalogue of dates and names, etc. It is intended as a field guide and for reference rather than to be read from cover to cover. Occasionally there is a comment about the setting of a church but on the whole little is said about their position or atmosphere. The amount of material given for a particular church in this book is not necessarily a true indication of how interesting or attractive the building may be. Notable features of a church or its graveyard may lie outside the scope of this book as outlined above. The gazetteer features Ordnance Survey grid references (these are the two letters and six digits which appear after each place-name and dedication) and is intended to be used in conjunction with the O.S. 1:50,000 scale maps. These are vital for finding the more isolated buildings.

Plans redrawn from originals in the author's field notes are reproduced to a common scale of 1:400. The buildings were measured in metres and only metric scales are given. For those who feel a need to convert three metres is roughly equal to ten feet. A system of hatchings common to all the plans is used to denote the different periods of work. On some pages there may be insufficient space for a key to the hatching to be shown. Where this is the case refer to another page. The plans should be treated with some care. There are some things difficult to convey on small scale drawings (e.g. stones of one period being reused in a later period, sometimes in a different location). Parts of some buildings can be difficult to date accurately. This volume contains proportionally less plans compared to some other churches books in the series. There is less variety in the planning of Cornish churches than in other parts of England and it was not thought necessary to give a large number of plans of entirely 15th and 16th century churches with essentially similar layouts.

ABOUT THE AUTHOR

Mike Salter is 45 and has been a professional author-publisher since he went on the Government Enterprise Allowance Scheme for unemployed people in 1988. He is particularly interested in the planning and layout of medieval buildings and has a huge collection of plans of churches and castles he has measured during tours (mostly by bicycle and motorcycle) of all parts of the British Isles since 1968. Wolverhampton born and bred. Mike now lives in an old cottage beside the Malvern Hills. His other interests include walking, maps, railways, board games, morris dancing, playing percussion instruments and calling dances with a folk group.

Copyright 1999 by Mike Salter
First published April 1999
Folly Publications, Folly Cottage, 151 West Malvern Rd, Malvern, Worcs WR14 4AY
Printed by Aspect Design, 89 Newtown Rd, Malvern, Worcs. WR14 2PD

The porch at Launceston Church

CONTENTS

Introduction	4
Further Reading	11
Gazetteer of Churches	12
List of other Anglican Churches	119
Manorial Chapels	119
Scilly Isles Churches	119
A Glossary of Terms	120

Inside the front cover is a map of churches in the gazetteer

INTRODUCTION

Cornwall has fine selection of early Christian relics. There are inscribed stones from the 6th to the 10th centuries, a large number of holy wells and fragments of over 300 early crosses, mostly small and plain, lying in and around churches, in fields and by the side of roads. There are also remains of several early monastic type settlements with dry-stone huts as at Tintagel. However, no remains of note survive of Saxon churches, not even at St Germans, where a bishopric was established by King Athelstan.

So much was replaced during Cornwall's boom period for church building in the later medieval period that the churches contain less work of the 12th and 13th centuries than most English counties. About fifty churches have remains of 12th century work in them but much of it is no more than a patch of masonry containing a single doorway or window. There is, however, a very fine series of Norman fonts, nearly half of the churches having a font earlier than 1200. Most parish churches of this period were small and simple as first built. They comprised a nave with a south doorway and sometimes also a north doorway also. On each side there would be one or two small round-headed windows with deep internal embrasures. In the east wall would be a round arch opening into a square chancel containing the altar. In some cases the altar was contained in a semi-circular space known as an apse. None still stand in Cornwall but one at Redruth is known from excavation.

A few Norman churches either from the start or as the result of slightly later expansion had more ambitious plans. Although the church at St Germans ceased to be a cathedral it remained one of Cornwall's greater parish churches. Of a substantial Norman church there remain a pair of west towers (a pair being a rarity in a parish church at any period), with a superb portal of many orders between them. The towers backed onto aisles with arcades of circular piers, two of these piers being the only parts to remain of the Norman church east of the west front. Other churches had just a single aisle. Arcades opening into such aisles, in each case on the north side of the nave, survive at Morwenstowe, North Petherwin and St Breward.

Churchyard cross at Michaelstowe

Norman tympanum at Egloskerry

Holy Well at Michaelstowe

One of the more complete Norman churches in Cornwall is that at Tintagel. It is a long, low building with the exceptional feature of an original Norman vestry north of the sanctuary. This church also has original transepts of unequal length. Transepts are unusually frequent in Cornwall, being present in about a quarter of the medieval churches. Most of them are of early date but precisely how early is usually difficult to say. No records of construction have survived and few of these transepts contain features allowing us to be sure whether they are 12th century, 13th century, or even early 14th century. The same is true of a number of early towers, which are sometimes placed in a transeptal position. At Blisland, Duloe, Morgan-in-Pydar and St Edonoc towers stand beyond the end wall of a transept, such a position being very rare elsewhere in England. In Cornwall towers are slightly less likely than normal to be placed in the traditional position at the west end of the nave. Gunwalloe, Gwennap, Lamoran, Launceston and Talland all have towers which are or were originally detached from their churches, this being another Cornish peculiarity rarely found elsewhere in England. Crossing towers set in the middle of cruciform churches are rare in Cornwall. A much repaired 13th century example remains at St Anthony-in-Roseland, and it seems there was a 12th century one at Crantock.

Although at least a quarter of the medieval churches retain fabric of the 13th century much of the work is fragments of little importance or uncertain date. Only St Ervan, St Anthony-in-Roseland and St Michael Penkevil, all cruciform, give an idea of what churches of that period looked like, although the last two buildings are now mostly Victorian reconstructions. Many plans in this book show chancels as having 13th century masonry, especially the eastern corners, but in fact there are rarely details allowing accurate dating. By the early 13th century the pointed arch had replaced the arch and windows took the longer form known as lancets. Later in the century these were placed together in two and threes with simple tracery above them. Original surviving examples in Cornwall are rare but a triple lancet window remains at Manaccan and twin lancets survive at Trevalga.

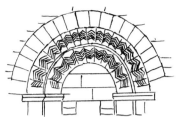

Norman arch at Liskeard

Doorway at Landewednack

Doorway at Cury

The early 14th century style is known as Decorated, with more complex forms of window tracery and the use of the ogival arch. Work of this period can be seen in many churches, especially North Hill, St Ives, St Michael Penkevil and Sheviock.

By the mid 14th century we have the beginnings of the style of church building that takes us through to the end of the medieval period and well into the 16th century. The Cornish developed a fondness for churches where the nave and chancel became a single chamber undivided except by a rood screen. On one side or both sides would be aisles running the full length of the church, nearly all the medieval churches having at least one aisle of this period. Sometimes the one side (usually the side facing the approach, which was more commonly the south) was rebuilt in this period but the other side retains older masonry, commonly with a transept. The contrast between the late medieval work often faced with granite slabs and the older work, usually of rough rubble, can be quite dramatic. Clerestories are rare and in a fully aisled church the three parts would be the same height, covered with wagon-roofs, with windows usually of three or four lights in the side walls, but much larger windows, sometimes of five or six lights, in the end walls. Some of the earlier piers are of square form with four attached half round shafts but the the most common type is of similar section but with the corners of the squares replaced by a concave curve. Most of the capitals are plain but the Devonshire type with a band of horizontal leaves also appears, whilst the piers at Fowey and Lostwithiel have no capitals at all. In the 14th century the arcade arches normally have two orders with chamfers. Later on concave curves replace the chamfers and still later a few churches have arches with more complex mouldings. By the 15th century standardisation was the order of the day, resulting in a great many churches that are all basically of similar appearance. The design of these churches makes them sometimes appear more spacious inside than they actually are. A comparison of the plans in this book with some of the other churches books in this series will show that despite being fully aisled many of the Cornish village churches are not all that large. The churches at Constantine, Gwinear, and St Ives are not huge even though they each have an outer aisle on one side, giving four parallel bodies. However there are large churches in the towns of Bodmin, Launceston and Truro. The last two display very fine early 16th century facades of sumptuous carving in granite.

Madron: pier capital

Poughill: pier capital

Late medieval towers in Cornwall are usually of two or three stages (although there are four stages at Fowey, Linkinhorne, St Buryan, St Columb, and St Ives), faced with granite slabs and having battlements and corner pinnacles at the top. Many towers are unbuttressed whilst others have buttresses set back from the corners. Buttresses actually at the corners, set either square or diagonally, are rare in Cornwall and usually indicate a date before the 1350s. Also usually indicative of a date before then are spires, which only occur at Cubert, Gerrans, Lostwithiel, Menheniot, Rame, St Anthony-in-Roseland, St Enodoc, St Ewe, St Hilary, St Keverne and St Minver. There were also once spires at Bodmin and Truro. In all there are over forty towers likely to be earlier than the 1360s. Cornish church towers were quite often built high so that they could be seen, and their bells heard, amongst a deeply incised landscape. That at Probus is the tallest and finest of them. As with the interiors the towers often look bigger than they actually are in simple plan form compared with towers elsewhere.

Sithney Church

Window tracery mostly appears in the larger end windows, windows in side-walls tending to be lower and of simpler form, often three lights with cusping to the four-centred heads of the lights, the tops of the windows either being flat or four-centred of a flattish shape. In the 16th century the round arch begins to replace the four-centred arch and tracery gradually dissappears. The late medieval style for towers and arcades continued well into Queen Elizabeth's reign, making close dating of some of the churches for which no building records survive quite difficult. Thus there is quite a bit of work which is Elizabethan in date, but not much of it is obviously Elizabethan in style.

Because granite does not flake and decay like sandstone and limestone the churches built of it have generally stood the test of time with less restoration than in churches elsewhere in England. The only real weakness with these buildings is that the jambs of windows are generaly formed from a single vertical slab bonded to the wall-face only by the strength of the mortar and in some places these have shown signs of movement. Such windows could easily be unobtrusively reset in a rebuilt wall. Not many new churches have been built since 1600 in Cornwall. A new church was erected at Falmouth in 1662-4, Helston has a church of 1751-61 and Redruth one of 1756, whilst St Enoder and St Eval have towers of 1711 and 1724-7 respectively and Werrington is mostly of 1742. Only about two dozen churches are entirely Victorian, most of them small and unimportant. Thus the overwhelming impression given by Cornish churches, especially when viewed from the outside, is late medieval work.

Porch at Tregony

Benches at Kilkhampton

Cornish churches have quite a good collection of old woodwork, mostly from the 15th and 16th centuries, and often with few hints of the Rennaissance even in the later work. Many churches retain old roofs and benches with motifs such as shields and scenes carved on the ends are common, with good collections being at Altarnun, Gorran, Kilkhampton, Laneast, Lanteglos-by-Fowey, Launcells, Morwenstowe, Mullion, St Ives, St Levan, St Minver and Talland. Miserichords, or stalls with folding seats with lips to support a chorister when standing, only survive at St Buryan. It became the custom for the chancel of a church to be divided off from the nave by a screen with a rood or image of the Crucifixion fixed over it. Sometimes there was a loft over the screen for the use of musicians and the performers of religious plays. The lofts rarely survive but their former presence is frequently indicated by the survival of a narrow stair leading up to it in a slight projection from the the outer wall. Among many old screens in Cornwall the best and least restored are at Laneast, St Buryan, St Ewe, St Levan and St Winnow. Old screens dividing off chapels and towers are also common. There are several Elizabethan and Jacobean pulpits, often with round arches and pilasters. Of older pulpits there are 15th century examples of wood and stone respectively at Camborne and Egloshayle (stone pulpits are uncommon) and a pulpit of c1530 at Mawgan-in-Pydar.

Of other furnishings to be noted there is medieval stained glass in several churches, the best preserved work being at St Kew, St Neot and St Winnow. A number of churches feature the royal arms either on a painted board or fashioned in plaster. Most of these relate to the period between Charles II's Restoration of 1660 and Victoria's accession in 1837. Several Cornish churches have a board giving the text of a letter written to the county in 1643 by Charles I thanking the inhabitants for their loyalty and help during the Civil War. One church, St Nectan, suffered serious damage during the conflict. Medieval wall paintings survive in a fragmentary state at Breage, Lanivet, Likinhorne, Poundstock and St Just-in-Penwith, a common scene amongst these being the Warning to the Sabbath-Breakers in which their tools of trade are shown around Christ's wounded body.

Font at St Ewe

Font at Ladock

Amongst some of the finest furnishings are the best of the series of well over 100 Norman fonts. A lot of them have not only a main supporting shaft but four corner shafts with heads and other motifs inbetween, Bodmin and Roche having the best of these. Many of those without the extra shafts still have heads at the corners. as at Altarnun, where there are rosettes inbetween. Fowey has the best of another group with hemispherical shaped bowls and decorative bands of crosses, etc. Egloshayle is the best of a final group shaped like a table top and having blank arcading. Later fonts are less important, although there is a fine 14th century example at Lostwithiel.

Font at Tregony

Font at Mawgan-in-Pydar

Brass at Constantine

Medieval effigies carved from stone are rare in Cornish churches. The best of a small 13th century group are at Little Petherick, Mawgan-in-Pydar and Ruan Lanihorne. From the 14th century there are another four plus two brasses. Of about twenty monuments of the 15th century all of them are brasses, i.e. with a figure or figures cut out of a sheet of brass upon which lines are engraved, and the sheet fixed into a stone in the floor, or on a tomb, or on a wall. The earliest brasses are the largest and best, the later ones tending to have a lot of hatching. Another dozen brasses are of the early 16th century, and a similar number are late 16th century, and there are a few effigies of stone. In the 17th century brasses become rarer, but stone effigies also eventually went out of fashion as well. Of over sixty monuments of that period noted in the gazetteer the majority are tablets. Incised slate slabs were particularly common in Cornwall during the 17th and 18th centuries, but there are also some tablets of the type with three dimensional architectural surrounds, urns, cherubs, symbols of death or of a profession. The gazetteer notes almost forty 18th century monuments, generally of these two types. There are good collections of monuments of different types at Fowey and St Michael Penkevil.

Effigy at Egloskerry

Tomb at Padstow

Pulpit at Liskeard

Tomb at Launcells

FURTHER READING

Cornish Church Guide, Charles Henderson, 1925
Norman Architecture in Cornwall, Edmund Sedding, 1909
Cornwall, Buildings of England series, Nikolaus Pevsner, 1951
The Story of Cornwall's Churches, S.V.Daniell, 1980s
Devon & Cornwall Notes & Queries.
See also periodicals such as: Cornish Magazine, Archeologia
Leaflets and/or pamphlets are or were available at the churches of:
   Blisland, Bradoc, Calstock, Forrabury, Lansallos, Landewednack,
   Lawhitton, Lezant, Madron, Maker, Mawgan-in-Meneage, Mylor,
   Perranuthnoe, Rame, St Columb Major, St Germans, St Mellion,
   St Just-in-Roseland, St Martin-by-Looe, St Michael Penkevil,
   St Minver, St Wenn, Stoke Climsland, Stratton, Talland,
   West Looe, St Mary (Isles of Scilly).

Lanteglos-by-Fowey

GAZETTEER OF CHURCHES

ADVENT   *St Adwena*   SX 105816

Only the arch remains of a former south transept removed in 1870. About that time the 13th century north transept with lancets was rebuilt. The nouth aisle with an arcade of five bays was added in the 15th century. The aisle east window has a flamboyant centre motif in the tracery. The west tower is unbuttressed, of three stages, and has eight pinnacles, the only instance of this in Cornwall. There are ceiled roofs, that in the porch having large bosses, one of which has three T-crosses. The south doorway has isolated fleurons on the jambs and voussoirs and tracery in the spandrels of the four-centred door-head. The plain round font is Norman.

ALTARNUN   *St Nonna*   SX 223813

The west tower is of three stages with buttresses set back from the corners. It is 32.5m high but does not dominate every direction, being set against a slope. The NW corner stair turret rises above the pinnacles. The aisles have five bay arcades and wide four-light 15th century windows with the pointed arches over pairs of lights. The east windows are of the same type. The piers, complete with their capitals and bases, are each carved out of a single piece of granite. There is a large Norman font with beaded faces at the corners and rosettes in between. The late medieval screen and the altar rail (Jacobean in style but dated 1684) both run across the whole width of the church. The set of seventy-nine 16th century bench ends are of some interest, the carved motifs including the Instruments of the Passion, St Michael, an angel with the inscription "Robert Daye, Maker of this Work" with an illegible date, a man with a cauldron, a fool, a bagpiper, a fiddler and angels holding shields.

ANTONY   *St James*   SX 398546

The sedilia and piscina and one window in the chancel are of about the time of the dedication recorded in 1259. The slate tower of two stages with diagonal buttresses and a corbelled-out parapet is 14th century. In the 15th century aisles were added, that on the south being the earlier and having straight-headed windows and an arcade of square piers with half-shafts. The pulpit has four carved panels of the Evangelists which look like Spanish work of c1500. The chest is from Tavistock Abbey. There is a fine brass depicting Margery Arundell, 1420, under a canopy with an ogival arch and finials. There are monuments or slates to many Carews, notably Richard, d1620, author of "A survey of Cornwall", Sir John, c1692, and two of his children, a portrait medallion of Mary, d1731, plus a monument to Admiral Graves, d1755.

BLISLAND   *St Protus and St Hyacinth*   SX 100732

The dedication is unique, Protus and Hyacinth being 3rd century martyred brothers. The main body and north transept remain of a Norman church, the north doorway being original and a font with concentric Vs and a herringbone moulding along the top. The west wall is strongly battered and has no doorway whilst the east end has three 13th century lancets. The six bay south arcade leans dramatrically to the south. It is 15th century as are the aisle and porch, the chapel east of the north transept with a four-light east window, the ceiled wagon roofs, a second font, and the tower added north of the north transept. The second stage of the tower is recessed and the third stage even more so with slim clasping corner buttresses. The south transept was rebuilt by Sir John Morshead in 1791 as his burial place but is now the vestry. There are Royal Arms of 1604, a late 17th century pulpit, a brass to Rector John Balsam, d1410, and a monument with six kneeling figures of the Balsam family dating from the 1620s.

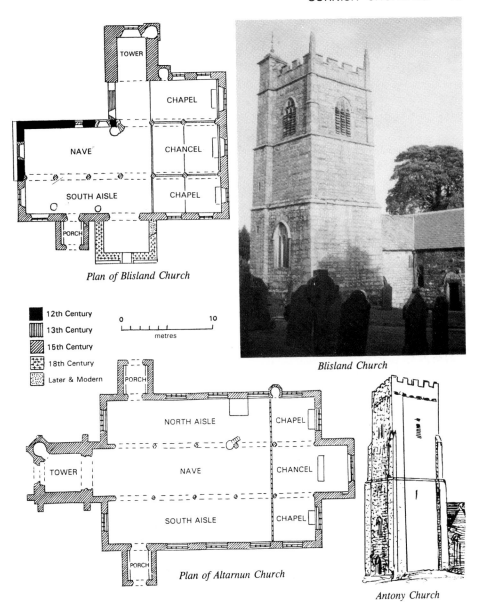

Plan of Blisland Church

12th Century
13th Century
15th Century
18th Century
Later & Modern

0 10
metres

PORCH

Blisland Church

TOWER
NORTH AISLE
CHAPEL
NAVE
CHANCEL
SOUTH AISLE
CHAPEL
PORCH

Plan of Altarnun Church

Antony Church

BOCONNOC   *Dedication Unknown*   SX 146606

The church lies behind the house and consists of a nave, a south aisle and porch, a
north chapel and a SW turret instead of a true tower. Parts of the roofs are old but
the six bay arcade has been much restored. Of greater interest are the contents: a
15th century font with tracery decoration set upon five supports in the 13th century
manner, a pulpit of 1629 with figures at the corners, part of an old screen, a set of
Royal Arms of painted plaster, and a kneeling figure of Penelope Mohun, d1637.

BODMIN   *St Petroc*   SX 073670

The Norman tower on the north side may originally have been set beyond a north transept. The former spire rising to 45m was destroyed in 1699. Most of the rest of the church was rebuilt in 1469-72, making it the largest parish church in Cornwall. The accounts survive and tell us that twenty masons were employed at 6d each per day. The total cost was nearly £270 but would have been much more but for the fact than many of the locals laboured on the work for nothing. The aisles are as wide as the nave and there are arcades of nine bays. The three eastern bays marking the chancel have lower arches. The arches dividing off these three eastern bays from the rest are an unusual feature for Cornwall. The church is all embattled with stair turrets and a two storey south porch with upper niches and a fan-vaulted lower stage. Restorations in 1814, 1867, 1888, and 1930 have replaced most of the windows and the roofs except for parts of that in the east end of the south aisle.

Inside the south door is an octagonal cresset stone with an eight-foiled depression in the top. There is a fine Norman font with corner shafts with busts of angels as capitals, interlaced and undercut foliage, scroll ornament and symmetrical beasts with trees of life between them. The aisle screens incorporate panels from the former rood screen and bench ends. The choir stalls and reredos of 1932 contain panels from the benches mentioned in a contract of 1491. The same document refers to the pulpit with fine carving and a base made up of fragments from the original choir stalls. Part of the top of a lantern cross in the churchyard also now lies inside the church. From the priory church has come the effigy of Prior Thomas Vivian, d1533. The tomb chest has figures of the Evangelists, cherubs with shields and balusters of Italian type showing the influence of the tomb of Henry VII at Westminster. There is also a slate slab to Richard Durant, d1632 and his wives and twenty children, and a fine incised slab to Peter Bolt, d1633. A foliated cross-slab lies outside the south wall. An ivory casket, probably that in which the relics of St Petroc were returned to the Prior of Bodmin in 1177 after having been stolen, was itself stolen in 1994.

Interior of Bodmin Church

Bodmin: Tower of Holy Rood Church

East of the church lies the ruined chapel of St Thomas Becket licensed for worship in 1377 and having a vaulted crypt underneath it. The chapel is a single chamber with a SW porch. It has a fine east window and a set of sedilia with cinquefoiled arches, next to which is an ogee-headed piscina, all 14th century. The Berry Tower beside the road to Helland north of the town is the ruined mid 15th century tower of the former parish church of the Holy Rood.

Sedilia in Chapel of St Thomas Becket at Bodmin

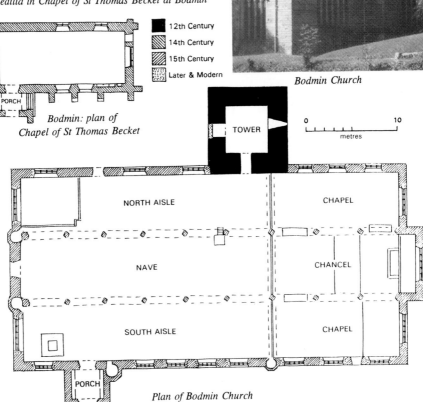

■ 12th Century
▨ 14th Century
▨ 15th Century
▦ Later & Modern

*Bodmin: plan of
Chapel of St Thomas Becket*

Bodmin Church

TOWER

0 ⌞ ⌞ ⌞ ⌞ ⌞ ⌞ ⌞ ⌞ ⌞ ⌞ 10
metres

NORTH AISLE

CHAPEL

NAVE

CHANCEL

SOUTH AISLE

CHAPEL

PORCH

Plan of Bodmin Church

BOTUS FLEMING   *St Mary*   SX 405613

The tower has diagonal buttresses and may be 14th century. The arcade between the nave and north aisle has octagonal piers with fleurons on the capitals. One pier has a niche for a statue on the west side and the adjoining piers also have brackets for smaller figures. The font has seven blank niches with pointed heads. The south side has been refaced. A sundial on the porch is dated 1787. Under a recess lies a much damaged effigy of a cross-legged knight, probably of the Moditon family.

BOYTON   *Holy Name*   SX 320920

The unbuttressed west tower is 14th century but has round-headed belfry windows of 1692-3. The nave and south aisle have a typical 15th century arcade between them and roofs of the same period. The oval font is Early Norman. The lower part remains of a screen of c1500.

BRADOC   *St Mary*   SX 162621

The church lies alone near woods. The north transept is 13th or 14th century but the arches between it and the nave are 19th century. An aisle with a five bay arcade was added on the south side in the 15th century, both nave and aisle having wagon roofs of that period. The base of the screen is probably of c1530-40 and the pulpit is Elizabethan. There are also bench ends with motifs such as Father Time, two figures of saints, and smaller saints on shields with their emblems on adjoining shields. The panels near the screen are of uncertain date and purpose.

Botus Fleming Church

Boyton Church

Bradoc Church

Interior of Breage Church

BREAGE   *St Breaca*   SW 618285

This is a granite 15th century church although restored in parts. The nave and aisles have seven bay arcades and there are transeptal chapels which are embattled like the rest. They have windows without cusping in the lights and may be later additions. The south porch has panelled jambs and buttresses. The tower has buttresses and grosteque heads and gargoyles on the top cornice below the battlements. On the north wall are original paintings of St Chrispher, the Warning to the Sabbath-Breakers, St Hilary, St Corentine and St Ambrose. Other saints appear in the embrasures of the south windows. A few pieces of original stained glass remain on the north side. The church contains a Roman Milestone referring to Marcus Cassianus Posthumus (258-68) and outside in the churchyard is the head of a Saxon wheel-cross.

BUDOCK   *St Budock*   SW 786324

The three stage west tower with diagonal buttresses may be 14th century. The 13th century south transept has one east lancet and a double-chamfer arch towards the nave on shafts with moulded capitals. A north aisle with a seven bay arcade and a south porch with panelled jambs were added in the 15th century. Only the base of the rood screen remains but there are Georgian box-pews. There is a brass depicting John Killigrew, d1567 and his wife, and also part of a monument with kneeling figures to Sir John Killigrew which was erected in 1617.

Porch at Budock

Calstock Church

Callington Church

CALLINGTON   *St Mary*   SX 358697

This church is all of the thirty years or so before the consecration of 1438, except for the outer north aisle added in 1882 by J.D.Sedding. The arcades are of four wide bays with square piers with four half-shafts and arches with concave chamfers. There is a clerestory with the windows set above the spandrels of the arcades. Externally this is mostly hidden by the aisle battlements. The wagon roofs are original and also the south door. The three stage west tower has set-back corner buttresses ending at the top of the second stage. polygonal projectings then rise from demi-figures of angels to end with pinnacles. The font has faces at the corners and rosettes in circles. Under a carpet is a brass with figures of Sir Nicholas Assheton and his wife, 1466. Rather finer is the alabaster monument to Sir Robert Willoughby de Broke, Steward of the Duchy of Cornwall, d1502. There is also a slab depicting Ann Holiday, d1753, kneeling. The Royal Arms of George III are dated 1811. In the churchyard is a worn late medieval lantern cross on a plain octagonal shaft.

CALSTOCK   *St Andrew*   SX 436692

The early 15th century north aisle has an arcade with square piers with half-shafts. The slightly later south aisle has piers of the typical Cornish type and arches with more complex mouldings. The three stage west tower is also 15th century. The windows are mostly lancets probably of early 19th century date except for the mullion-and-transom type windows at the east end. The Edgcumbe family chapel of 1558 contains monuments to Piers, d1666, and Jemima, Countess of Sandwich, d1674, the latter having two mourning figures and a large coronet. The Royal Arms are dated 1816 although the heraldry is correct for earlier in George III's reign.

CAMBORNE   *St Martin and St Meriadocus*   SW 645400

The outer south aisle and porch are of 1878, although the porch bears a sundial of 1797 over a medieval arch. Otherwise the church is mostly 15th century with aisles having five bay arcades, the two eastern arches on each side being slightly lower. There are four and five-light windows with four-centered heads to each light and no tracery. The west tower has set-back buttresses. There is a roodloft staircase on the north side. The altar contains an altar slab from Chapel la at Troon with a key-design on the edge and lettering referring to the donor Leuiut. Heraldry dates the pulpit to c1480. The reredos is of 1761. There a monuments to Sir William Pendarves, d1726, by James Paty of Bristol, and Anne Acton, d1780, by Francis Robins of Bath.

CARDINHAM   *St Meubred*   SX 123687

The east end of the chancel has been rebuilt since being damaged during the Second World War. A vestry has been added against the chancel north wall, which is 13th century and contains a recess and a lancet, possibly reset since it lies right against the east end. Otherwise the church is mostly 15th century with a north aisle of five bays, a south aisle of six bays (the last bay flanks part of the chancel), a small south porch, and a west tower with set-back corner buttresses. The arcades have piers of the usual Cornish type and the aisle windows are of three lights except those facing east. There are original wagon roofs and fine bench ends, and Royal Arms of Charles II dated 1661. Of c1400 is the small brass to Rector Thomas Awmarle. He is shown in civilian dress complete with an anelace or short ceremonial sword. There is also a monument of c1700 to the Glynn family. In the churchyard is a fine 9th or 10th century cross with panels, plaitwork, interlace and an inscription on the shaft.

Cross at Camborne

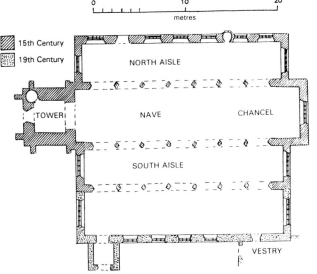

0   10   20
metres

15th Century
19th Century

NORTH AISLE

TOWER   NAVE   CHANCEL

SOUTH AISLE

VESTRY

Plan of Camborne Church

Brass at Cardinham

Constantine Church

COLAN   *St Colanus*   SW 867613

The church stands alone by some trees. The south transept and the south walls of the nave and chancel are 13th century. The chancel inclines to the south. The north side has a 15th century aisle with a three bay arcade towards the nave. An arch divides the aisle from a two bay north chapel. The south porch is also late medieval. Only the base survives of the rood screen and the west tower was rebuilt in 1879. There are brasses to John Cosowarth, d1575 and his family, and to the Bluett family with twenty-two children, c1580.

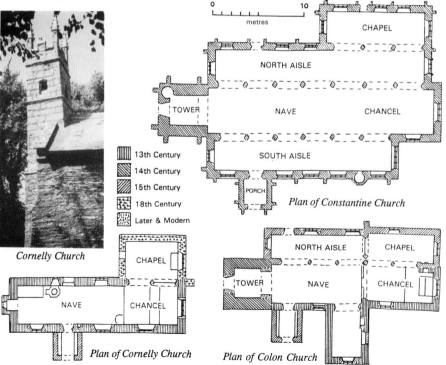

Cornelly Church

13th Century
14th Century
15th Century
18th Century
Later & Modern

Plan of Constantine Church

Plan of Cornelly Church

Plan of Colon Church

CONSTANTINE   *St Constantine*   SW 721291

Despite some restoration this is essentially a late 14th to early 15th century church of granite blocks set in a commanding position above a creek of the Helford River. The south aisle is of six bays and has a porch with set-back corner buttresses. The polygonal stair turret marks the position of the former screen. The north aisle has seven bays but still does not quite extend to the chancel east wall. Its three eastern bays are flanked by an outer chapel with set-back buttresses and windows of three lights with late 14th century type tracery. The piers are all square with four attached shafts. The west tower has set-back buttresses with heads at the top, panelled pinnacles, lozenges on the top cornice, and an arch towards the nave with shafted responds. The brass of Richard Gerveys, d1574 and family is a palimpsest with the top part of a 14th century Flemish brass on the reverse.

CORNELLY   *St Cornelius*   SW 916452

The slate lower stage of the slim west tower with a tiny west lancet is 13th century. The granite upper stage dramatically leaning to the west is probably later. The nave north wall also has one 13th century lancet. The south windows and porch with a wagon roof are 15th century. The north chapel is 18th century. The font seems to be rustic 17th century work and of the same period is the pulpit with coats of arms. There is a portrait bust of Jane Reeves, d1783.

COTEHELE   SX 424685

Above a 20m high cliff above the River Tamar is a late 15th century chapel marking the spot where Richard Edgcumbe escaped from Sir Henry Trenowth in 1483 by jumping down into the river. The three-light east window, two-light side windows, the west doorway, the ceiling and four bench ends have survived restorations of 1620 and 1729.

Screen at Crantock Church

Crantock Church

CRANTOCK   *St Carantoc*   SW 790606

The nave and transepts are Norman and there was a central tower until it collapsed in 1412. The north transept has pilaster corner buttresses. A new chancel is assumed to have been built after c1236 when Bishop Brewer of Exeter created a college here. The existing chancel rising higher than the nave is 14th century and has chapels with lean-to roofs and arcades with octagonal piers. The roughcast west tower with corner buttresses is probably early 15th century. Of that period are the fragments of a figure of the Virgin plus two saints inside the tower south wall. The font is Norman but is dated 1474 when it was recut. Most of the screen is of the time of the restoration by Sedding in the 1890s.

CREED   *St Crida*   SW 935472

The west tower of three stages with set-back buttresses was rebuilt in 1734. The nave north wall looks Norman and the north transept is 13th century but with late 14th or 15th century windows. The transept has a Norman pillar piscina with chevrons on the pillar under a trefoiled arch. Of the 15th century are the south aisle with a five bay arcade with piers of the usual Cornish type, parts of the original wagon roof, fine south and east windows, and the south porch with fluted jambs and a pointed tunnel-vault with transverse arches. The chancel piscina and the aisle west window are 14th century. The 13th century font has two shallow blank niches with pointed heads on each of the eight sides. Only part of the rood screen remains. There is an engraved slate to Thomas Ducys, d1559, and his wife and son, d1602, and there a tablet to John Hugh, d1749.

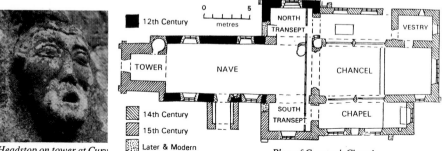

Headstop on tower at Cury

Plan of Crantock Church

CROWAN *St Crewenna* SW 646345

The church is all of granite and was much restored in 1870-2 when a 17th century south arcade was replaced by one of the usual Cornish type, the aisle rebuilt, and a big organ-chamber was added east of it. The three narrower eastern bays of the north arcade are Elizabethan. The western three bays of this arcade have piers with capitals holding shields of arms relating to a St Aubyn marriage of 1398. The unbuttressed tower is of three stages. There are brasses to Geoffrey St Aubyn, d1420, and his wife, Geoffrey St Aubyn, and his wife, c1490, and Thomas St Aubyn and his wife, c1550. There is also a small standing figure of Colonel Thomas St Aubyn, c1650, and monuments to two Sir John Aubyns, d1714 and 1772.

CUBERT *St Cubert* SW 786577

The west tower with slightly set-back buttresses and a broach-spire was rebuilt in 1852 but the arch towards the nave is clearly original work of c1300. The nave north doorway and the arch towards the north transept are of about the same time. In the 15th century a six-bay south aisle was added, plus a new south transept projecting from the aisle. The transept south wall has a tomb recess. There are original wagon roofs in the chancel and aisle. Some windows are of Street's restoration of 1846-9 but the transept end windows are old. The 13th century font has rosettes and stars on a bowl with five supports, the outer four having shaft-rings. The pulpit is made from old carved bench ends. There is a slate to Arthur Lawrence and his sons d1669 and 1699. On the tower west wall is an inscribed stone probably of the 7th century.

CURY *St Gunwalloe* SW 677213

The Norman south doorway has one order of columns ornamented with keys and chevrons. The tympanum has interlaced rings with chevrons and beads. There is a south transept with a squint formed by having an octagonal pier replace the corner of where the chancel and transept walls would meet. Of the early 15th century is the north aisle with a six bay arcade of Cornish standard type. There are horizontal leaves on the abaci of the piers. The aisle outer wall has a staircase which led to the former loft on a rood screen. The unbuttressed west tower has a NW stair-turret rising above the pinnacles. The west doorway and window above have heads as label-stops. The Norman font has corner shafts and star or rosette medallions between.

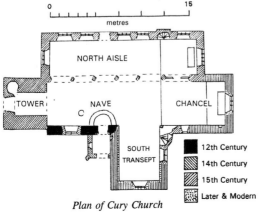

Plan of Cury Church

Font at Cury

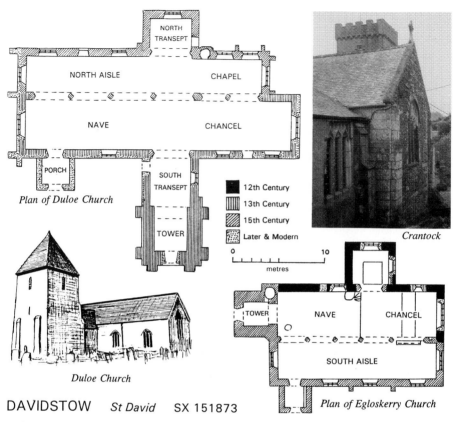

Plan of Duloe Church

12th Century
13th Century
15th Century
Later & Modern

0   10
metres

Crantock

Duloe Church

Plan of Egloskerry Church

DAVIDSTOW   *St David*   SX 151873

This is a late medieval building with three east windows each of five lights. The tall west tower with set-back buttresses has a plain parapet. The church was heavily restored in 1875 by Hine of Plymouth, the north side being rebuilt, so the only ancient details and furnishings are bench ends in the south aisle depicting a saint, a lion, a bagpiper, and a kneeling man who was probably the donor of the benches.

DULOE   *St Cuby and St Leonard*   SX 234581

The south transept and the tower beyond it are 13th century. A 15th century top stage of the tower was replaced in the 1860s by something similar to the original roof. The tower has an original south doorway and an arch towards the transept which was blocked at an early date. The transept has an arch towards the nave which matches the arches of the 15th century north arcade of four bays. The north chapel was built to house the tomb and effigy of Sir John Colshull, d1480. His effigy is poor when compared with the rich carving on the two arches between the chapel and the chancel. The chapel screen may be be formed from parts of the original rood screen and bears the Colshull arms. The chapel is embattled with pinnacles, distinguishing it from the rest of the building. There are engraved slates in the chapel to Anna Coffyn, d1592 and two other women of the same period with their children, and to John Killiow, d1601, and Mary Arundell, d1629. A relief of a woman holds a portrait medallion of Henry Bewes, d1793.

EGLOSHAYLE *St Conan* SX 001719

Two north windows are of c1300 and the north wall and doorway and the north transept may be still older, but the rest is 15th century. A south aisle with a six bay arcade and porch were then added but the intended north aisle was never completed. The lofty tower has set-back buttresses and a doorway with roll-mouldings in the form of snakes. It was donated by John Loveybond. The south aisle has a wagon roof with supporting angels and fine windows, that to the east being of five lights. The octagonal pulpit of Caen stone with emblems of the Passion and emblems referring to John Loveybond is 15th century. There is a Norman font with blank arcading on the sides. A large white and grey marble monument with a bust commemorates Dame Barbara Molesworth, d1735.

EGLOSKERRY *St Keria* SX 273866

The church lies in the middle of the village. The north wall and the north and south doorways are Norman. The blocked north doorway has a tympanum with a dragon trying to bite its own tail. The south tympanum now lies inside the church and has a lamb and cross. Also Norman are the font with cable moulding, the piscina in the chancel formed of a block capital with palm-leaves on a short shaft and probably the masonry of the north transept. Of the 15th century are the three-stage west tower without buttresses and the south aisle with a five bay arcade. A worn effigy of Sir Guy de Blanchminster, d1404 in civilian dress was moved from the north transept in 1886 to a recess at the south aisle east end, the feet being hacked off to make it fit.

Egloshayle Church

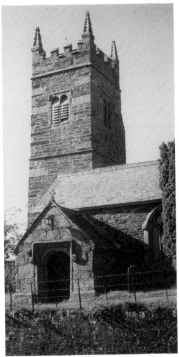
Egloskerry Church

FALMOUTH   *King Charles Martyr*   SW 809326

The church was built in 1662-4 with Sir Peter Killigrew as the main sponser. It was then 20m square with granite columns with plaster Ionic capitals dividing it into a nave and aisles with panelled roofs. The two tiers of windows are of late medieval type. An oblong west tower was added in 1684. A chancel added then was replaced by a longer chancel with a Venetian east window in 1813. Galleries inserted at the turn of the 17th and 18th centuries were mostly removed in a restoration of 1896 by Sedding. The pulpit contains 16th and 17th century carving and there is a credence table of 1759 with the Killigrew arms. The old glass in one window came from Italy in the 19th century. In the vestry is an alabaster relief of the Flagellation. The oldest monuments are those of Thomas Corker, d1700, and Richard Lockyer, d1789.

FEOCK   *St Feoca*   SW 825384

The existing church is 19th century except for the arcade and south doorway which are 15th century. There is a Late Norman circular font with a frieze of two tiers of diagonal crosses and circles with trees of life, all perhaps recut, and a pulpit with four late 16th century carved Flemish panels. The low, pyramidal-roofed 13th century tower of the old church stands nearby. It had a low pointed arch towards the nave. Also in the churchyard is a cross with a crucifixion and circular head, a Saxon type, although the foliated cross on the back suggests a 13th century date.

Falmouth Church

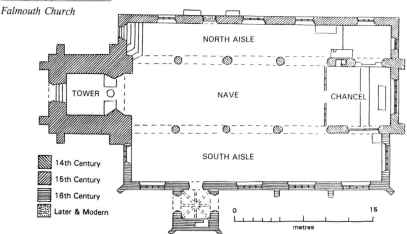

TOWER

NORTH AISLE

NAVE

CHANCEL

SOUTH AISLE

14th Century
15th Century
16th Century
Later & Modern

0   15
metres

Plan of Fowey Church

Forrabury Church

FORRABURY *St Symphorian* SX 095909

The church lies on a bare hillside above Boscastle. The short nave and and the cup-shaped font with a diagonal criss-cross pattern are Norman. There is a north aisle with an arcade of depressed two-centred arches on thick columns inserted in 1867. Two big granite slabs cover the south porch. The short embattled tower with plain pinnacles looks medieval but is actually of 1750. The pulpit is Jacobean. There is a cross south of the churchyard.

Fowey Church

FOWEY *St Nicholas* SX 126516

The arcades of five double-chamfered pointed arches rising without capitals from octagonal piers must be part of the work dedicated in 1336. Of the late 15th century are the outer walls of the wide aisles, the fine carved wagon roof, the south porch with an octopartite vault and arches to the east and west, plus the west tower of four stages with set-back buttresses and bands or ornamentation on the plinth and stringcourses and pannelled pinnacles.The four-light south windows and five-light east window with colonettes in their inner jambs may be as late as the early 16th century. The Norman font has rosettes in circles and an upper border of crossed zig-zag lines. The hexagonal font is of 1601. There are brasses to two 15th century civilians, one acommpanied by his wife, and to John Rashleigh, d1582, and Alice Rashleigh, d1602. John Rashleigh, d1610 is depicted lying on a chest in a ruff and beret. Another monument to this family dates to 1683.

Detached tower at Feock

GERMOE   *St Germoe*   SW 586294

The nave south wall, the chancel, the south transept with one rounded-headed west window, the scalloped stoup in the north transept and the font with three heads are all Norman. Several windows are 14th century and the north aisle with an arcade of low piers of standard Cornish type is probably late 14th century. A matching arch leads into the north transept which may also be Norman, but truncated by the addition of the aisle. Similar arches divide off the south transept, but the pier is placed diagonally. The 15th century south porch has a gable resting on two animals and crowned by a crucifix. The peculiar little building called St Germoe's Chair on the churchyard wall entered by a twin arch with a circular pier and containing three seats with shafts separating blank arches is probably 15th century.

GERRANS   *St Gerent*   SX 873352

The 14th century west tower of slate has diagonal buttresses and an octagonal spire with a ring of quatrefoils halfway up. The rest of the church was rebuilt in 1849 by William White, although he is said to have used old parts and to have not altered the design of the building except for adding a vestry. The south arcade with square piers with four attached shafts looks original. There is a Norman font with four blank niches on each side of a square bowl. A few medieval bench ends remain, plus a monument of 1718 by Weston of Exeter to Edward Hobbs.

Gerrans Church

Font at Gerrans

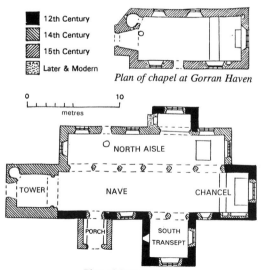

	12th Century
	14th Century
	15th Century
	Later & Modern

Plan of chapel at Gorran Haven

0   10

metres

NORTH AISLE

TOWER   NAVE   CHANCEL

PORCH   SOUTH TRANSEPT

Plan of Germoe Church

GOLANT   *St Samson*   SX 120552

The church was consecrated in 1509 and most of the features could well be of about that time. It has a low embattled west tower and there is a holy well in the corner between it and the porch. The nave has a fine wagon roof and the aisle has a ceiled cradle roof. The arcade between them is of seven bays with low piers of the usual type. Both parts have straight-headed windows. The pulpit and stalls contain carvings from former bench ends with motifs such as two crowned heads on castles, a fool's head, and the arms of Colquite family. One window has 15th century stained glass figures of St Anthony and St Samson. The marble head of Christ looking up looks like Italian Baroque work. There is a slate plate to Edmund Constable, d1716.

GORRAN HAVEN   *St Goranus*   SX 013416

This is a small chapel tucked in amongst houses. It has a slender west tower and 15th century windows plus a south doorway with a fine arch over which is a niche. Much of the building, however, dates from the rebuilding of 1885.

GORRAN   *St Goran*   SW 999423

The oldest features are the Norman font on five supports with corner faces and other motifs in between, and the 13th century north transept arch and blocked north doorway with heads as label stops and on the apex. The early 15th century south aisle has three-light south windows, a four-light east window containing fragments of original stained glass, and an arcade of eight bays of two-centered arches on piers of an unusual section with moulded capitals. Renaissance motifs indicate a 16th century date for the set of fifty-three bench ends. Some also bear initials of donors and the Instruments of the Passion. There is part of a foliated cross-slab and also a brass of a kneeling woman of c1510. By the tower arch is the indent of another brass with a border inscription and shields. The monument of Richard Edgcumbe of Bodrugan, d1604 was either imported from Italy or made in England much later.

Font at Gorran Church   *St Germoe's Chair, Germoe*

Gunwalloe Church

GRADE   *Holy Cross or St Grada*   SW 713144

The church is mostly of 1862. Of the small medieval church the only remains are the west tower, parts of the nave with two original doorways, that on the north being blocked, the 13th century font with short corner shafts and stair, rosettes and other motifs in circles, plus the brass depicting James Erisey, d1522 and his family.

GULVAL   *St Gulval*   SW 485318

The unbuttressed west tower with three stages built of granite blocks is of 1440. Probably of about the same date are the octagonal piers of the south arcade with angels holding shields on the capitals, a motif also found on the font. In the drastic restoration of 1892 by J.P.St Aubyn the north aisle was entirely rebuilt and the south aisle given new windows. One old window head and parts of two crosses lie by the SW corner outside. A damaged monument has kneeling figures of John Davills, d1627 and Arthur Harris, d1628. There is also a monument to William Harris, d1766.

GUNWALLOE   *St Gunwalloe*   SW 660205

The church lies close to the shore and has a pyramidal-roofed detached early tower built into the native rock. The church is late 14th to early 15th century and has arcades of five bays and a chancel extending slightly further east, plus a south porch with panelled jambs. This sounds ambitious but the scale is all quite modest with windows of just two lights on the north but of three lights on the south. Fixed on the inside of the north and south doors are panels with painted apostles from the 15th century rood screen. The south aisle and porch have old wagon roofs.

Detached tower at Gwennap

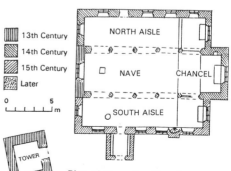

IIII 13th Century
NNNN 14th Century
//// 15th Century
Later

0   5
L__I__I__I__I__I m

Plan of Gunwalloe Church

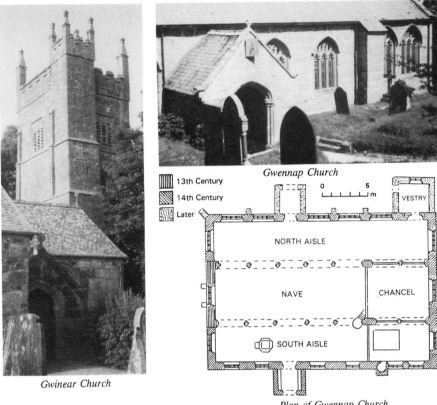

Gwennap Church

▦ 13th Century	
▨ 14th Century	
▩ Later	

0 ___ 5 m

VESTRY

NORTH AISLE

NAVE   CHANCEL

SOUTH AISLE

Gwinear Church

Plan of Gwennap Church

GWENNAP *St Wennapa* SW 738401

The pyramidal-roofed detached tower may be 13th century masonry, the church having masonry of that period at the SW corner. In the south aisle is a 14th century trefoil-headed piscina. Most of the south side and the arcades are 15th century. The rest was partly rebuilt in 1862.

GWINEAR *St Gwinear* SW 595374

The west tower with set-back buttresses and a NE stair turret rising above the battlements and pinnacles was being erected in 1441. The bell-stage has straight-headed windows. The chancel has an east window of five lancets of c1300 and other windows with intersecting tracery. The north aisle runs the length of the church but the south aisle starts two bays from the west end, the arcade on this side having piers with four major and four minor shafts, the arches being almost semicicular, i.e. probably 16th century. The north arcade has piers of the usual Cornish type but with horizontal leaves on the capitals towards the west, whilst the eastern piers have capitals with four angels holding shields. The arcade of the Arundell Aisle forming an outer aisle or chapel flanking this part also has capitals with this motif. The south aisle windows have four lights with four-centred heads and no tracery. The pulpit, lectern and kneeling desk are all made up from medieval bench ends. Only the base remains of the early 15th century rood screen.

Helland Church

GWITHIAN   *St Gocianus*   SW 587413

An early oratory here was excavated in the 19th century but is buried by the sands again. The church was rebuilt in 1866 by Edward Sedding except for the west tower with panelled pinnacles. A few 15th century features are reset in the lychgate. The font is carved with a snake, rosette, and a cross in medallions. It may be medieval but seems to have been recut.

HELLAND   *Dedication Unknown*   SX 075710

The four bay arcade of typical Cornish type is 15th century and there is a cup-shaped font perhaps of the 13th century, plus a worn early 16th century incised slab to one of the Calwodley family. The other features are 19th century.

HELSBURY   SX 083796

Only buried foundations now survive of this lonely chapel.

HELSTON   *St Michael*   SW 658278

The Earl of Godolphin had this church erected in 1751-61 to a design by Thomas Edwards. The nave has five round-headed windows and a gallery on three sides with short iron columns and a flat ceiling. There is a lower chancel and a west tower with pilasters instead of true buttresses and obelisks instead of pinnacles. The south porch with pilasters and a stair up to the gallery was added in 1830. Within the porch is a brass to Thomas Bougins, d1602, and his family. There is a brass chandelier of 1762.

Helston Church

Jacobstow Church

HERODSFOOT   *All Saints*   SX 215605

In the church of 1850 lies a 14th century font with a frieze of foliage scrolls on the upper rim of the round bowl. It came from the ruined chapel of St Martin at Respryn.

ILLOGAN   *St Illogan*   SW 672440

Only a 14th century grantite tower with diagonal buttresses remains of the old church. The church of 1846 by St Aubyn contains a recut font with corner faces, a brass of c1605 to James Basset and his wife, a relief with kneeling figures from a monument to the Reverend John Collins, d1684, a tablet with two putti to Mary Collins, d1743, a monument to Francis Basset, d1769, and many later monuments to members of the Basset family.

JACOBSTOW   *St James*   SX 199958

The church is essentially 15th and 16th century work but contains a Norman font with faces at the corners and six-petalled flowers in niches in between. The arcades are of four bays with piers of the standard type. The embattled granite porch has a tunnel-vault. The granite tower is unbuttressed and has carvings on the plinth. The north door is original, the pulpit is made up of old bench ends and the communion table with bulbous legs serving as the altar is Elizabethan.

Doorway at Kilkhampton

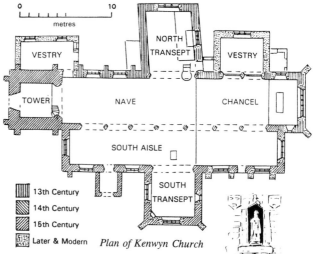

0   10
metres

NORTH TRANSEPT

VESTRY

VESTRY

TOWER

NAVE

CHANCEL

SOUTH AISLE

SOUTH TRANSEPT

||||| 13th Century

\\\\\ 14th Century

///// 15th Century

Later & Modern

Plan of Kenwyn Church

KEA   *All Hallows*   SW 844417 & 810426.

The church of 1895 by Fellowes Prynne lies on the site of a church of 1802 by James Wyatt and contains a Norman font on five supports with heads at the corners and on the sides two trees of life, a cross and a lion. It is from the old church of which only the embattled three storey tower with diagonal buttressses now remains. To it a small mission church was added in 1863.

Doorway at Kilkhampton

KENWYN   *St Cuby*   SW 819459

The church lies high above Truro. The nave north wall and north transept are 13th or 14th century. The south aisle with an arcade of seven bays with standard piers and four-centred arches is 15th century, as is the west tower of three stages with set-back buttresses. The late 15th or early 16th century arch dividing off the north transept has figures of a bishop and an angel on the capitals.

KILKHAMPTON   *St James*   SS 253114

Much of the church, including the series of bench ends carved with motifs such as the Instruments of the Passion, a flagon and chalice, thirty pieces of silver, a lantern, a lance, lantern and halberd, and a cock on a pillar, dates from the period 1524 to 1580 when John Grenville was rector. The south porch is dated 1567. There are aisles with arcades of seven bays with piers of standard type with four centred arches, original wagon roofs, and a west tower with set-back buttresses. The only obviously older feature is the fine south doorway of four orders with chevrons and fir cones, heads and stylized leaves on the capitals. The Royal Arms were made by Michael Chuke, a local carver who made the monuments of John Warminster, 1700, Richard Westlake, 1704, and John Courtis, 1705. The monument to Sir Bevill Grenville, killed in a naval battle in 1643, was only erected in 1715.

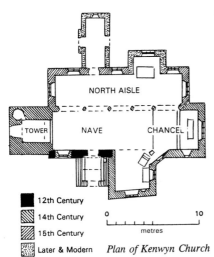

12th Century
14th Century
15th Century
Later & Modern   *Plan of Kenwyn Church*

0   10
metres

Kenwyn Church

LADOCK   *St Ladoca*   SW 894 510

Parts of the church said to have been consecrated in 1268 remain on the north side. The south aisle with a six bay arcade with slim piers of standard type and finely moulded arches is 15th century. Of the same period are the north chapel and the west tower of three stages with set-back buttresses, plus the south porch with a wagon roof and decorative carving. The face in a boxed frame over the south doorway may be Norman. The chancel was much restored by G.E.Street in 1862-4 and its fittings are of that period. The circular font with an upper border of two tiers of crosses and trees of life in circles below is Late Norman. The lower part of the screen remains and the lectern is made up from old bench ends.

LAMORRAN   *St Moran*   SW 878418

This small cruciform 13th century church was mostly rebuilt by William White in 1845. The building in the SW corner of the churchyard could be part of a former detached tower. In the church are a Norman font on five supports with corner faces, old doors, and a big monument to John Vernan, d1758, and his wife.

LANDEWEDNACK   *St Winwallo*   SW 712127

This is the most southerly church on the mainland of England, lying by an attractive village near the Lizard. The Norman south doorway has columns of serpentine and chevrons and circles on the arch voussoirs. It is protected by a rib vaulted porch, probaby 14th century, like the unbuttressed west tower and the south transept and chancel linked by a squint formed by replacing the corner between them with a pier. This pier matches those of the five bay arcade of the late 14th or early 15th century north aisle. The long vestry and the organ recess are 19th century, although the latter has a reset medieval window. The chancel east window has reticulated tracery. The font stands on short columns and has an inscription relating to Richard Bolham, rector of the church from 1404 to 1442. This church was the scene in 1670 of the last sermon preached in the Cornish language.

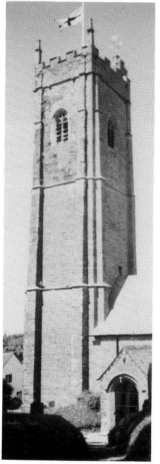

Landrake Church

LANDRAKE   *St Michael*   SX 374605

The font with corner faces and large rosettes in circles, and the south doorway with colonettes are Norman. Of the 15th century are the lofty west tower with set-back buttresses and a polygonal NE stair-turret rising above the pinnacles, the north aisle with a four bar arcade, the pinnacled, shallow porch, and arch to the south transept. The arcade piers are unusual as the attached shafts have a three-quarter round section. A squint connects the transept with the chancel and the rood-loft staircase. There is a small brass to Edward Cowtney, Lord of Wootton in Landrake, d1509, and there are two slate plates of 1607 on the chancel north wall.

LANDULPH   *St Leonard*   SX 432615

The church is essentially late medieval and has five bay arcades with octagonal piers and arches with two concave chamfers plus a west tower with a polygonal stair turret and set-back buttresses lower down, but with diagonal buttresses higher up. The north aisle has a fine wagon roof and there is an octagonal font on five supports. The base of the rood screen is original, and there are several bench ends carved with a number of motifs such as a boar's head, a fox, a goose, a rabbit and a hawk or eagle. The fine family pew of 1600 with linenfold carving and heraldry belonged to the Lower family of Clifton, and there is a monument to Sir Nicholas Lower, d1655. An inscription records the burial here in 1636 of Theodore Palaeologus, a descendant of the medieval Christian Emperors of Byzantium, who died at Clifton.

■	12th Century
▨	14th Century
▧	15th Century
▤	17th Century
▦	Later & Modern

0 —————— 10
metres

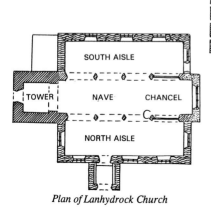

Plan of Lanhydrock Church

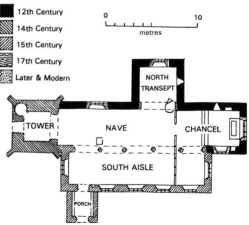

Plan of Laneast Church

Landulph Church

LANEAST *St Sativola Virgin or St Michael* SX 228840

The nave north wall, the north transept and the chancel are Norman, and so is the font with corner faces and six-petalled flowers in circles on the sides. The north transept has an east window with original jambs, whilst the north window is a small 13th century triple lancet. The west tower with diagonal buttresses at all four corners is 14th century. A top stage was added in the 15th century when the granite south aisle and porch were added, both with fine wagon roofs. There are a nearly complete set of late medieval benches with the ends carved with coats of arms and motifs such as knots and stars. The rood screen also survives and some stained glass in the chancel with figures of Christ crucified, St Christopher and St Catherine. South of the church is a small 16th century building containing a holy well.

LANHYDROCK *St Hyderoc* SX 084636

The small granite church lies behind the fine 17th century manor house. It has four bay arcades with standard piers and an unbuttressed west tower of three stages. The windows are late medieval in style but may actually be 17th century. There are plaster Royal Arms of 1621. There is a monument to Lady Essex Speccott, d1689. In the churchyard is a Saxon cross with interlace and foliage scrolls.

LANIVET *St Nevet* SX 039642

The exterior looks all 15th century with a variety of Perpendicular style windows and a lofty west tower with set-back buttresses. The six bay arcades may be 14th century, like the font with traceried panels, and a dedication is recorded in 1318. Both arcades have circular piers with four attached shafts, the south arches being double chamfered, whilst the northern ones have concave chamfers. Until the 19th century there were wall paintings of such subjects as the Warning to the Sabbath-Breakers. The large Norman capital has probably come from Bodmin Priory. There is a slate plate of 1632 to John and Richard Courtenay.

LANLIVERY   *St Bryvyth or Brevita*   SX 080590

The church has a commanding position above the Fowey estuary and the lofty 15th century west tower is visible from afar. It has set-back buttresses below but at the bottom of the third stage octagonal pinnacles are corbelled out on angels and beasts. The north transept is perhaps 14th century, having a window of that period. Another is reset in the west wall of the 15th century south aisle with an arcade of six wide bays on slim piers of standard section. The aisle and south porch have original wagon roofs. The large octagonal font with shields in quatrefoils is 15th century but there is also a damaged Norman font. There is a monument to Mary Cotes, d1758. A sundial on the porch is dated 1715.

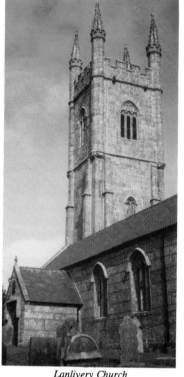

Lanlivery Church

LANREATH   *St Manarch and St Dunstan*

SX 181569

Nothing remains which can be associated with the dedication of 1321 but the nave north wall and north transept are probably Norman, the period of the cup-shaped font with chevrons, plaits and palmettes. The rest is late medieval, comprising a west tower with set-back buttresses, a south aisle with an arcade of five bays with standard piers with ornamented capitals, the south porch, the fine wagon roofs, that in the nave with bosses, and the rood screen with painted saints on the bottom panels. There was a careful restoration by G.Bodley in 1887, and the screen was restored in 1905. The chancel stalls with carved figures are partly of c1500 and partly Jacobean. The pulpit is Elizabethan, the font-cover is Jacobean, and in the transept are Jacobean bench ends and an Elizabethan altar table. There is a rustic wooden monument with kneeling figures of Charles Grylls, d1623 and his wife.

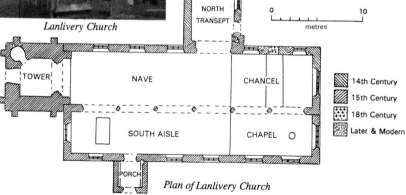

Plan of Lanlivery Church

Font at Lanreath Church

Font at Lanlivery Church

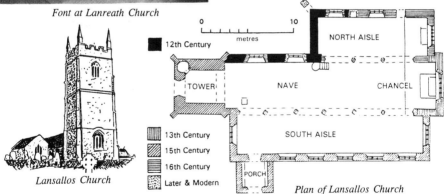

Lansallos Church

12th Century
13th Century
15th Century
16th Century
Later & Modern

0   10
metres

NORTH AISLE

TOWER   NAVE   CHANCEL

SOUTH AISLE

PORCH

Plan of Lansallos Church

LANSALLOS   *St Ildierna*   SX 173516

Of the pre-15th century church the west wall of the north transept and the north wall of the nave survive together with a square Norman font with a tree of life and fleur-de-lis. The south aisle has a six bay arcade with standard piers and three light windows with renewed tracery and a porch, both parts having old roofs like that of the nave. One of the roofs was damaged during an air raid in 1941. The north aisle forms an east extension of the former transept and has a three bay arcade and a 16th century window and another of domestic type of the 17th century. The west tower has diagonal buttresses at all four corners. There are many early 16th century benches with carved heraldic arms, heads, etc, and two Jacobean vestment cupboards. There are damaged effigies of a 14th century knight and lady of the Hywys family, and a slate slab carved by Peter Crocker to Margery Smith, d1579.

LANTEGLOS-BY-CAMELFORD   *St Julitta*   SX 088823

This is the original parish church of Camelford despite being 2km to the SW. The chancel and north transept retain Norman masonry and the unbuttressed west tower with a NE stair turret and heads on the hoodmould of the west doorway is 14th century. Of the 15th century, and of granite, are the south aisle with a six bay arcade with depressed four-centred arches, and south porch and the chancel east wall with a five light window with flamboyant tracery. Some original stained glass remains in some of the heads of the south windows. The commandment boards are Elizabethan, making them unusually early. In the churchyard is a 10th century inscribed pillar.

LANTEGLOS-BY-FOWEY   *St Willow*   SX 144515

The jambs of the south doorway are Norman. The XP stone built into the doorway is much earlier. The church was appropriated in 1284 to the Hospital of St John at Bridgwater and was rebuilt in the 14th century. It has a nave and west tower which are both wider than usual and aisles of differing widths. All have original roofs, those of the nave and south aisle being moulded. The arcades have octagonal piers and have five bays with each bay wider than is often the case in Cornwall. The tower has massive walls and has double chamfered arches towards both the nave and the aisles. Of the 15th century are the aisle windows and the rood loft staircase on the south side, whilst the porch may be a 17th century rebuilding. The south aisle east window has some old stained glass. The 13th century font bowl with stiff-leaf foliage lies on a Purbeck base with moulded capitals and bases. There are many bench ends of c1500 and also some Jacobean pews with coats of arms. The altar table of 1634 was donated by one of the Mohuns. There are brasses of c1440 and c1525 to Thomas de Mohun and John Mohun and his wife respectively, and there is an indent of a third brasss to a man and wife of c1520. The north aisle has Georgian box pews.

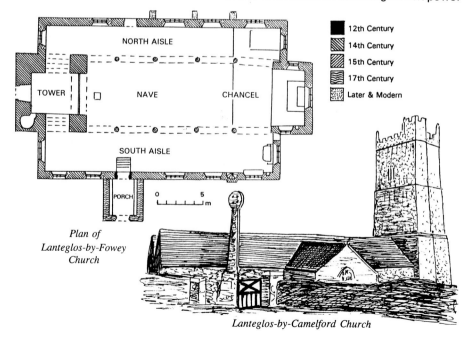

NORTH AISLE

TOWER   NAVE   CHANCEL

SOUTH AISLE

PORCH   0   5   m

	12th Century
	14th Century
	15th Century
	17th Century
	Later & Modern

*Plan of
Lanteglos-by-Fowey
Church*

Lanteglos-by-Camelford Church

Lanteglos-by-Fowey Church

LAUNCELLS   *St Swithin*   SS 244057

The unbuttressed west tower has very lofty corner pinnacles. The whitewashed interior with a plaster wagon roof over the nave has arcades of five bays with tall slim shafts of standard section with fleur-de-lis crenellations on the capitals and four-centred arches. The north arcade is of granite and slightly the later of the two. There are over sixty carved bench ends with abbreviated representions of the Passion such as the table with a flagon and loaves for the Lord's Supper, a flagon, dish and towel for the Washing of the Feet, an open coffin and spice boxes for the Resurrection and footprints and a cloud with feet and a rope end for the Ascension. In the chancel are 15th century tiles made at Barnstable with motifs such as fleur-de-lis, tudor roses, lions, and a pelican. The altar table is Jacobean and there is an Early Norman font with cable mouldings. The faded painting of the Sacrifice of Isaac on the south aisle west wall is 16th century. There is a monument with a semi-reclining effigy of Sir John Chamond, d1624.

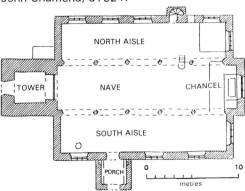

Plan of Launcells Church

Royal Arms in Launcells Church

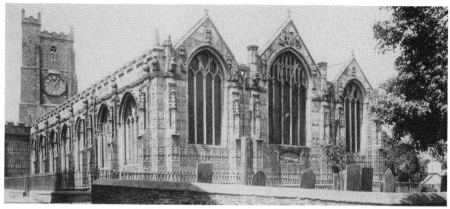

St Mary Magdalene's Church, Launceston

LAUNCESTON *St Mary Magdalene* SX 333847

This sumptuous church of granite was erected in 1511-24 at the expense of Sir Henry Trecarrel. The arcades of eight bays have circular piers with four groups of three attached shafts. The fifth bay from the west is wider with depressed four-centred arches, hinting at transepts which do not actually exist. The east window is of five lights and the others have four lights. The exterior is a mass of carved motifs, with quatrefoils, coats of arms and fleur-de-lis on the plinths, and tracery, more coats of arms and letters above. The buttresses too are ornamented. There are palm leaves by the windows and roses in the spandrels, a scroll ornament above, and then parapets with roses, thistles and pomegranates. The east end has a recumbent figure of Mary Magdalene below the window. There are kneeling figures there, most of them angels playing instruments. The royal arms appear at the top of the east gable. The south porch is of two storeys and is dated 1511 with the arms of the Trecarrel and Kelway families. There are also reliefs of St George and St Martin. The intended west tower was never built. Instead there are 20th century vestries at the SW connecting the church to a late 14th century tower on a different axis and having set-back buttresses. This is all that survives of the original chapel-of-ease, the parish church then being St Stephen-by-Launceston. The pulpit and font are also of the 1520s, there are carved Royal Arms of George III, and there is an organ front of the 18th century, but the wagon roofs are renewed. There are parts of a monument of c1650 with kneeling figures and other monuments to Captain Philip Piper, d1637, Sarah Rudole, 1667, and Granville Piper and Richard Wise, c1730.

LAUNCESTON *St Thomas* SX 333847

Norman are the tympanum built into the porch and the large font with corner faces and rosettes in circles. The lower parts of the small west tower are 14th century. The nave and chancel in one and the south aisle and porch are 15th centurty. The aisle has an arcade of five bays with standard piers, a staircase for a former rood loft and windows are three lights, except for the four-light east window. The chancel east window is of five lights. The north windows and the north vestry and organ chamber date from the restoration of 1874. The tower screen has 16th century linenfold panels. There are old wall paintings at the south aisle east end. The south door has 13th or 14th century ironwork.

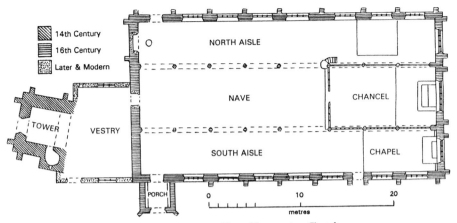

14th Century
16th Century
Later & Modern

NORTH AISLE

NAVE

CHANCEL

TOWER

VESTRY

SOUTH AISLE

CHAPEL

PORCH

0   10   20

metres

Plan of Launceston Church

Cross-head, Launceston churchyard

Porch at St Mary Magdalene's, Launceston

Tower, Lewannick

LAWHITTON   *St Michael*   SX 355824

The 15th century south porch with an old wagon roof lies close to the tapering south transeptal tower of the 13th century. The north aisle has an arcade of five bays with standard piers and straight-headed windows. The Norman font has corner faces and there are some old bench ends. The pulpit dated 1665 looks older. There are monuments to Robert Bennet, d1683, and Richard Coffin, d1796.

LELANT   *St Uny*   SW 548377

The aisles are the same width as the nave and have 15th century windows. The porch, the diagonally buttressed west tower and most of the arcades are 15th century also. The second arch from the west on the north side is Norman with a round pier and a half-round respond, the latter now part of a full pier since a plain pointed arch was provided later to link the Norman arcade with the tower. The other piers are square with four demi-shafts and have large horizontal leaves, a motif common in Devon. The south doorway has fleurons on the jambs and voussoirs and tracery in the spandrels. The octagonal font on nine supports is probably late medieval. There are kneeling figures of William Praed, d1620, and his family.

LESNEWTH   *St Michael*   SX 131904

The church lies on a steep hillside with a road at roof-level closeby on the north. Only the west tower with a north stair turret with tiny quatrefoil-shaped loops survives of a medieval church which had Norman transepts on both sides until rebuilt in 1865.

Lelant Church

LEWANNICK   *St Martin*   SX 276808

The four light east window is of the type where two lights are united under one arch. The three light east windows of the aisles and one south window are original but the other windows are probably 18th century. The south arcade was renewed after a fire in 1890 but otherwise the church is all late medieval with arcades of five bays with standard piers, but with an extra narrow arch on the north side. Both porches are original and there is a rood staircase on the north. The west tower has set-back buttresses lower down and polygonal pinnacles above. The west doorway has fleurons on the jambs and voussoirs, and flowers and scrolls in the spandrels. The window above has a crocketted ogival canopy and side finials. The large Norman font has unusual carved motifs such as a coil and a pentagram. One stone in the church and another outside have inscriptions partly in Roman letters and partly in the Ogham system of lettering used in the 5th to the 7th centuries. There is also a cresset-stone with seven cups.

LEZANT   *St Briochus*   SX 338791

The north wall is 12th or 13th century and has a doorway with a plain chamfered arch and a small cusped lancet. Other early parts are the chancel east buttresses and twin SE lancet and the Norman font with the corner faces later hacked off to make an octagonal bowl. Of the later medieval period are the west tower, the arcades of four bays with standard piers, the south aisle wall with original windows and the ceiled wagon roofs of the nave and both aisles. There are several monuments to the Trefusis family, including an altar tomb in the south aisle east end, a plate with kneeling figures and a reclining effigy of a 17th century lady.

Lesnewth Church

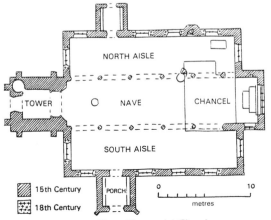

Plan of Lewannick Church

Lezant Church

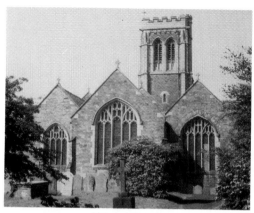

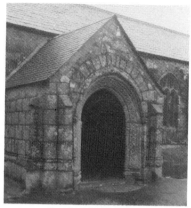

Liskeard Church

Porch at Linkinhorne

LINKINHORNE   *St Melor*   SX 319736

The church is entirely faced with granite ashlar blocks and is late 15th to early 16th century. The west tower was probably the gift of Sir Henry Trecarrel (see Launceston). It is 36m high but not conspicuous from afar as the church is low lying. There are five bay arcades with granite piers of standard section having foliage on the capitals and four-centred arches. The porch entrance has a figure of eight ornament, more a Celtic motif than a late Gothic one. In the south aisle is an altar slab with five crosses. The 13th century century font has a square bowl with narrow pointed blank arches. There are a few late medieval bench ends and the top of the aisle windows have some old stained glass. Revealed during the restoration of 1891 were part of a Norman capital and the wall paintings in the south aisle showing the Seven Corporeal Works of Mercy with Christ under a canopy and fragments of what are thought to be the Seven Deadly Sins. Near the village lies a small 15th century building containing the Holy Well of St Melor.

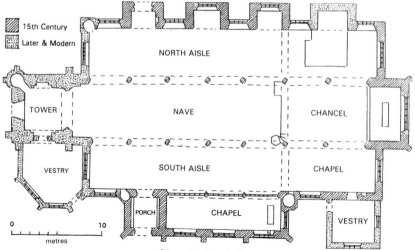

Plan of Liskeard Church

Old print of Liskeard Church

LISKEARD   *St Martin*   SX 254644

This is the second largest parish church in Cornwall, being 42m long. Essentially late medieval, but much restored in 1878-9 and 1890, etc, it has a nave of five bays and a lower chancel of two bays with the unusual feature for Cornwall of a chancel arch between the two parts. There are aisles and porches on both sides and a Lady Chapel of 1428-30 forming an outer aisle at the east end of the south side. The north aisle dates from the 1470s. The thirteen consecration crosses on the aisle walls are unique in Cornwall. The arcades have standard piers and are not high compared with the width of the nave. The south porch has an upper room with niches externally. The north porch is one of three bay-window type projections on the north side, each with battlements and tunnel-vaults with three transverse arches. Originally there may have been two west towers but there was only one by 1627 when it was rebuilt, although it required further repairs in 1675. The present tower with massive foundations going down to solid rock 4m below ground dates from 1903. It incorporates Norman fragments including a window high up and a blocked and partly renewed doorway or two orders both with chevrons. The plain font is probably 14th century. The pulpit is dated 1636. None of the many monuments are of great age or importance. There were several chantry chapels in the church including those founded by Edward Kemp the Elder and Thomas Clemens. By 1310 there was also a chapel in the park of the Earls of Cornwall 1km to the west, but it was abandoned after the Reformation and nothing seems to remain of it.

LITTLE PETHERICK   *St Patrock*

The church was rebuilt by William White in 1858 for the rector, Sir Hugh Molesworth and a north chapel was added c1916. Older relics are the 15th century font, some bench ends, two bells, and a 13th century foliated cross slab with a head to Sir Roger Lemporu. There is also a collection of old vestments and altar furniture from Italy and Spain donated by a Mr Riley, spouse of one of the Molesworths.

LOOE   *St Mary*   SX 256532

The parish church of East Looe was rebuilt by G.E.Street in the 1850s and later. Nearby is a chapel, also mostly Victorian but with the lower part of the tower old.

LOOE   *St Nicholas*   SX 254532

This small church serving West Looe is mostly of 1852 and 1862 with an arcade formed of timber from a wrecked ship, but the piscina is 14th century and the south wall and windows are 15th century. A chapel was founded here by 1330. After the Reformation it became a guildhall and was later used as a school.

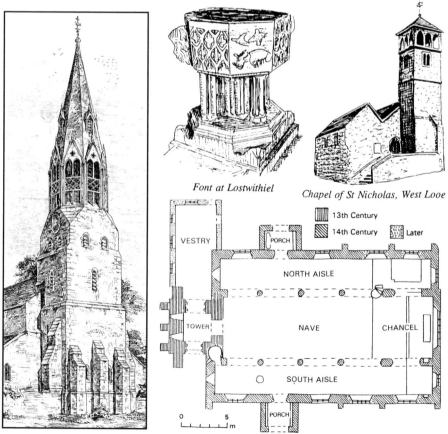

Font at Lostwithiel

Chapel of St Nicholas, West Looe

13th Century
14th Century   Later

VESTRY
PORCH

NORTH AISLE

TOWER   NAVE   CHANCEL

SOUTH AISLE

PORCH

0   5 m

Lostwithiel Church

Plan of Lostwithiel Church

Lostwithiel Church

LOSTWITHIEL   *St Bartholomew*   SX 105598

The west tower is 13th century with a 14th century broach spire with dormer windows and an octagonal screen at its foot with two lights, quatrefoil tracery and a gable on each side. A public passage ran north-south through the tower basement until 1878. The rest of the church is also 14th century with an aisled nave of four bays with octagonal piers without capitals, a chancel with narrower and lower arcades and a south porch. There is a clerestory of triple lancets set above the spandrels, perhaps renewed in the 17th century. There is a very fine five-light east window. The south doorway has colonettes with shaft-rings and a hoodmould on head corbels. There is also a splendid 14th century font with figures in panels. The alms box of 1645 inscribed W.T.Maier takes the form of a standing figure with a shield. An alabaster panel depicts the Flaying of St Bartholomew. West of the porch are two external tomb recesses. The many monuments inside include a brass to Tristram Curteys, d1423 and two Elizabethan wall-tablets.

Luxulyan Church

Ludgvan Church

LUDGVAN   *St Ludgvan and St Paul*   SW 506331

The chancel masonry and north window may be of the period just before the re-dedication recorded in 1336. The west tower with set-back buttresses may be 14th century but was heavily restored in 1888. It has corbelled-out pinnacles and heads like gargoyles below the battlements, and the arch to the nave has panelled jambs. The rest of the church is 15th century but the south aisle with its six bay arcade is slightly earlier than the north aisle with its four bay arcade. The piers have four major and four minor shafts. The Norman font has scalloped sides and a moulding at the top plus a cable-moulding below. There is a rustic monument to John South, d1636 and his family, and a brass inscription to Christopher Borlase, d1749.

LUXULYAN   *St Ciricius and St Julitta*   SX 052581

This is a large church built of big ashlar blocks of granite, i.e. all late medieval. The unbuttressed west tower has a very high NE stair turret. The west window contains bits of old stained glass. There are arcades of six bays with standard piers but with the capitals different on each side. Parts of the wagon roofs are old. The embattled south porch has a tracery panelled pointed tunnel vault. The Norman font has corner faces, trees of life and dragons. Nearby is a small building with a moulded doorway which contains a holy well.

MABE *St Laud* SW 757325

The granite church lies alone above a reservoir and is mostly of the restoration of 1866. Original are the unbuttressed west tower of three stages and the south porch with cable decoration and a pattern of a lily in a vase up the archway jambs and along the arch. The inner doorway of limestone has leaf-scrolls on two orders of jambs and voussoirs and decorated spandrels. Similar motifs appear on the tower west doorway. The octagonal piers have capitals evidently designed to fit piers of the Cornish standard type. On either side of the reredos are fragments of a 15th century alabaster altar showing the Annunciation, the Nativity and the Last Supper.

MADRON *St Madern* SW 454318

This is the original mother-church of Penzance and is a granite building of some size. The single sedile and piscina in the chancel and perhaps also the south arcade with four major and four minor shafts are of the period just before the re-dedication recorded in 1336, whilst the tower is probably rather later. The 15th century north aisle has an arcade with taller piers with decorated capitals, both arcades being of six bays. The south aisle was then rebuilt, perhaps wider than before. Old parts are incorporated in the wagon roofs. Two south windows have carved head keystones. The south porch is refaced or rebuilt. Parts of the rood screen still remain and there is a Jacobean tower screen. In the south aisle is a carved panel with a group of nine angels. There are several late medieval bench ends with pairs of shields with beasts on top. The altar rails are early 18th century. The monuments include a brass to John Clies, Mayor of Penzance, and his family, 1623, slate plates depicting John Maddern, d1621 and Thomas Fleming, d1631 and their families, plus kneeling figures of the Reverend Duke Pierce and his wife, 1720, a late date for such a monument. There is also a 6th or 7th century inscribed stone. 1km NW is the ruined 14th century baptistry of St Madron still retaining its altar, and with a holy well beside it.

Mabe Church

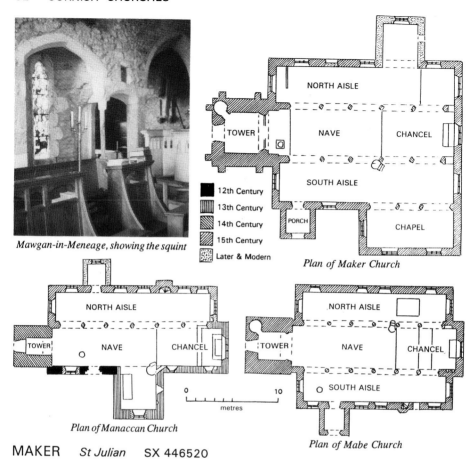

Mawgan-in-Meneage, showing the squint

- ■ 12th Century
- ▥ 13th Century
- ▧ 14th Century
- ▨ 15th Century
- ▦ Later & Modern

Plan of Maker Church

Plan of Manaccan Church

Plan of Mabe Church

MAKER   *St Julian*   SX 446520

The church lies alone and is all late medieval, only the Norman font with corner faces and snakes transferred here from St Merryn being older. There are five bay arcades with piers of Cornish standard type. The outer south aisle forming the Edgcumbe family chapel has an arcade with slight differences betraying a later date. The tower has set-back buttresses replaced by pinnacles at the third level. It was used by the Royalists as a strongpoint but captured by Parliamentary troops in 1644. There is a monument to Sir Richard Hunt, d1787 and there are many monuments to the Edgcumbes, although the only one of note is that of Richard, Lord Edgcumbe, d1758.

MANACCAN   *St Manacca*   SX 764250

The Norman south doorway has three orders of columns and fluted voussoirs. The top of a Norman shaft has also been discovered where the south transept joins the nave. The transept and chancel are connected by a squint and both have 13th century windows, with triple lancets in the chancel east wall. The 15th century north aisle has a rood-loft staircase and a six bay arcade with piers of standard type. The north doorway now leads into a Victorian vestry. The unbuttressed west tower of slate with heads as label-stops on the west doorway is 14th century.

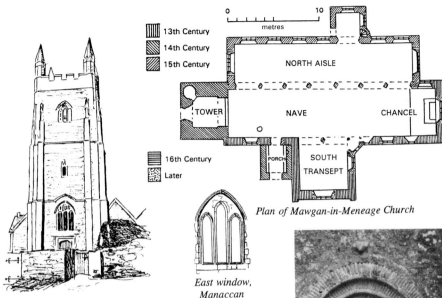

⊪ 13th Century	
⊠ 14th Century	
⊘ 15th Century	
▤ 16th Century	
⬚ Later	

NORTH AISLE

TOWER   NAVE   CHANCEL

PORCH   SOUTH
TRANSEPT

Plan of Mawgan-in-Meneage Church

Maker Church

*East window,
Manaccan*

MARHAMCHURCH   *St Marwenna*   SS 224037

The south transept is probably Norman. A late 14th century north aisle as wide as the nave and with a low arcade with standard piers has absorbed the former north transept. The nave and aisle both have old wagon-roofs. The west tower has diagonal buttresses and a polygonal NE stair-turret. There is a 17th century pulpit with a tester. There are also Royal Arms and a cresset stone. The window reset high up in the aisle west wall with a cusped head, a transom, and the lower part divided by a mullion may be a relic of an anchorite's cell built for Cecilia Moys in 1403-5.

Doorway at Manaccan

MAWGAN-IN-MENEAGE   *St Mawgan*   SW 709251

The chancel has two late 13th century cusped lancets and a three-light east window of c1340. A squint formed by a passage with a pier taking the place of the corner joins the chancel to the south transept with an arcade of two bays with a pier of standard Cornish type. This matches the 15th century seven bay arcade. The aisle north windows look 15th century but the west and east windows are clearly 16th century, the latter being of five lights. A small transeptal chapel on the north side contains the rood-loft staircase in one corner. The south doorway is 15th century but the porch adjoining the transept could be late 14th century, the likely period of the transept east window and perhaps also the unbuttressed west tower with shafted responds on the tower arch with angel-capitals. The octagonal font has corner shafts. In the south transept are effigies of a knight and lady of c1300. There is an inscribed stone perhaps of the 10th century, known as the Mawgan Cross.

Interior of Mawgan-in-Pydar Church

MAWGAN-IN-PYDAR *St Mawgan* SW 878659

Of the 13th century are the nave north wall, the north transept with a squint towards the chancel, and perhaps the base of the tower beyond the 15th century south aisle. This aisle has absorbed a south transept to which the original tower was attached, and east of which a south chapel with a two bay arcade was added in the late 14th century. A short piece of wall connects that arcade with the four bay arcade of the aisle, which has a contemporary south porch. The tower now appears 15th century in its present form with set-back buttresses and a NE stair turret. The nave west window has intersecting tracery of c1300. The chancel NE corner was rebuilt when a vestry was added in the 19th century and the windows of the transept and nave north wall are also Victorian. There is a Norman font on five supports with corner faces and chevrons and shields. The pulpit of c1530 has panels with Intruments of the Passion. The Arundell arms appear on the cornice of the rood-screen. There are many 15th century bench ends with pairs of shields with monograms, Instruments of the Passion, etc. In the south chapel is a worn brass to an early 15th century priest and there are fragments of other brasses to the following members of the Arundel family: George and wife, d1573, with part of an early 16th century Flemish brass on the reverse; inscriptions and shields of Jane, d1577 and Mary, d1578; Cecily, d1578, also with an earlier foreign brass on the reverse, and an unknown late 16th century man. There is a lantern cross in the churchyard.

Mawnan Church

MAWNAN   *St Maunanus and St Stephen*   SW 788272

The church lies among trees far from the village above the mouth of the Helford river. The 13th century chancel has an original piscina and one lancet. The west tower and two windows in the north aisle are probably late 14th century. The arcades with standard piers may also be of that date. There is a 15th century font and four painted panelled of saints remain of the rood screen.

MENHENIOT   *St Lalluwy*   SX 288628

The west tower with set-back buttresses, small windows, and an octagonal spire rising from within an embattled parapet on a corbel table is 14th century. The north aisle is perhaps late 14th or early 15th century and the south aisle with more elaboration of the arcade arches and capitals is later. There are fine ceiled wagon roofs. The fine brass inscription to Sir Ralph Carmynow, d1386, is the earliest brass in Cornwall. Of several monuments to the Trelawney family the most notable are those of Jonathan, d1674, and Edward, Dean of Exeter, d1726.

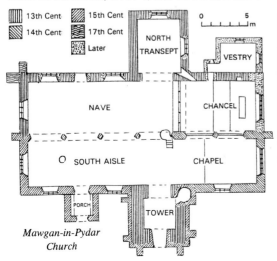

Mawgan-in-Pydar Church

Cross-head at Mawgan-in-Pydar

Mevagissy Church

MERTHER   *St Cohan*   SW 863448

This small church has now fallen into ruin. The north wall is Norman, with two original window embrasures, one now having a 14th century opening. The thin and heavily diagonally buttressed west tower is 14th century. Many windows look early 16th century and have hoodmoulds. The collapsed south arcade had Cornish standard piers. In a niche north of the altar there was a small figure of St Anthony.

MEVAGISSY   *St Peter*   SX 013453

The unbuttressed west tower has been rebuilt shorter with a saddleback roof after part of it collapsed. The south transept has a 14th century south window and of perhaps the same date is the trefoil-headed piscina in the nave. The north aisle has an arcade with Cornish standard piers but with decorated octagonal abaci. The circular Norman font has rosettes, a herringbone moulding above and chevrons below and a cable moulding on the base. There are reclining effigies one behind and above the other of Otwell Hill, d1617 and his wife, and a slate with kneeling figures of Lewis Dart, d1632 and his family.

MICHAELSTOW   *St Michael*   SS 205154

The unbuttressed west tower with a NE stair-turret is probably 14th century. The arcades have Cornish standard piers, four piers on the south side having large horizontal leaves on the capitals. This side has five bays but the north side is shorter at the east end, with only four bays because of an earlier anchorite's cell on the north side of the chancel where a stone with a quatrefoil opening still remains. There are original wagon roofs. The south doorway has fleurons on the jambs. Only the base of the font is old. There are a few old benches with shields on the ends. There are many slate plates such as that of Jane Merifield, d1663 with two standing figures. There is a tall early cross with a pierced circular head in the churchyard.

Michaelstow Church

Minster Church

MINSTER   *St Merteriana*   SX 013453

This is the parish church of Boscastle lying 1.5km to the SW in a dip in the hills. It was probably at the restoration of 1869-71 that the incomplete west tower was given a saddleback roof. There are 15th century aisles with arcades of four-centred arches on Cornish standard piers but 13th century windows survive in the chancel. The cup-shaped Norman font has diagonal criss-cross lines. There are monuments with small kneeling figures to a couple of 1611 and William Cotton, d1656, and his wife, and there is also a monument to John Cotton, d1703, plus many slate plates.

MITHIAN   *St Peter*   SW 746472

The church was mostly rebuilt by William White in 1861 and the lofty tower is a rebuild of 1928, but the arcade is medieval, and also the font and south doorway.

MORVAH   *St Bridget or St Morwetha*   SW 403355

The church is mostly of 1828 but has a 14th century west tower with a blocked doorway. Another blocked medieval doorway survives on the north side. Despite the central position of the tower to the wide main body it appears that the latter was originally divided by an arcade into a nave and north aisle.

MORVAL   *St Wenna*   SX 260566

The church lies close to the house and has evidence of 13th century work in the chancel and a south transept. The 15th century north aisle has an original roof and an arcade with Cornish standard piers with the capitals decorated with horizontal leaves. There is an unbuttressed west tower of slate, either 14th or 15th century. The almsbox is 17th century. There are kneeling effigies of Walter Coode, d1637 ad his wife. The children are allegorically expressed by fruit growing out of branches issuing from the adults, skulls above some of them showing that they died young.

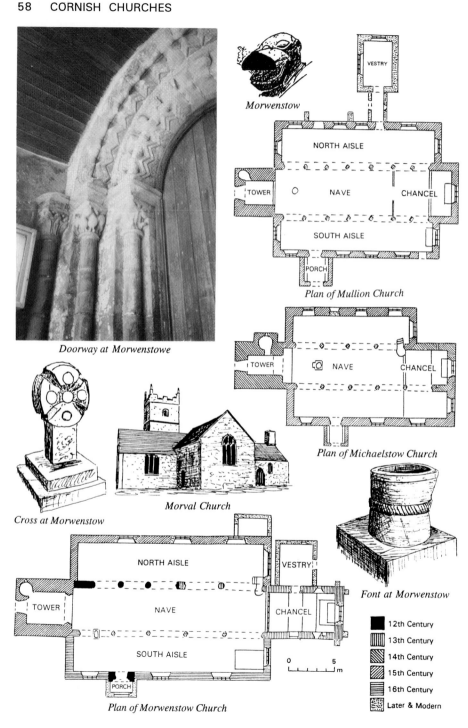

Doorway at Morwenstowe

Morwenstow

Plan of Mullion Church

Plan of Michaelstow Church

Cross at Morwenstow

Morval Church

Font at Morwenstow

Plan of Morwenstow Church

12th Century
13th Century
14th Century
15th Century
16th Century
Later & Modern

0   5
          m

MORWENSTOW *St John the Baptist* SS 205154

The church has a reset Norman south doorway with columns and chevrons. The original outer order now forms the arch of the porch outer entrance and has beads of men and beasts. Three bays of the north arcade are also Norman with arches decorated with chevrons and beakheads on circular piers with capitals with scallops and other motifs. There are grotesque heads of a ram and a pig boldly projecting from the spandrels between the arches. Further east on the north side are two bays of the 13th century with double-chamfered pointed arches on circular piers. The south arcade has Cornish standard piers. One bay is dated 1564 with initials on the capitals and abaci but that must refer to a repair, the rest probably being a generation or two earlier. There are original wagon roofs. The unbuttressed west tower facing the sea is 14th or 15th century. There is an egg-shaped Norman font with a cable moulding at the foot. The 16th century bench ends have Early Renaissance motifs. The chancel north wall has a faint painting of St Morwenna.

MULLION *St Melina* SW 678193

The church is essentially late medieval with only the 13th century octagonal font with blank trefoiled arcades and a serpent being obviously older. The unbuttresssed west tower has heads forming the label-stops of the west doorway and a small crucifixion relief above the upper window. There are aisles with arcades of Cornish standard design with original ceiled wagon roofs and doors. The church has a fine collection of old bench ends probably of the 1530s or 40s. There are Instruments of the Passion and initials and motifs such as a jester, a monk, and two cherubs with a chalice and barrel. The lectern has two panels with sibyls of the same period, and some original parts remain in the rood screen. There are carved Royal Arms of Charles II.

South doorway at Mullion

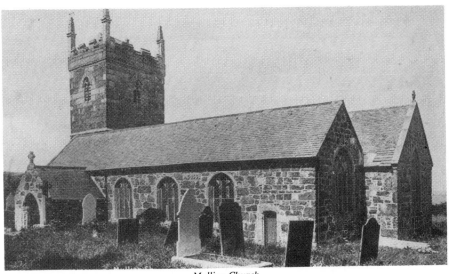

Mullion Church

Benches in Mullion Church

MYLOR   *St Melorus*   SW 820353

The church lies above a creek and has Norman work in the nave and north transept. The original north doorway has a Maltese cross in the tympanum and chevrons up the jambs and across the lintel. Another Norman doorway with one order of colomns and a cross on the tympanum has been moved from the nave south wall to the west end of the nave. The 15th century south aisle has an arcade of six bays of standard Cornish type. The fine south porch has a doorway with openwork tracery and panelled jambs. The octagonal font decorated with crosses lies on a 13th century base and shaft. There is an octagonal pillar piscina. There is a fine Elizabethan pulpit close to a well preserved rood screen inscribed "IARYS IONAI JESW CREST". In the churchyard lies a tall Saxon cross with incised circles and concentric circles.

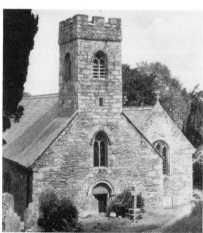

Mylor Church

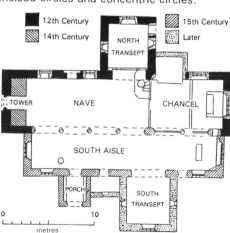

12th Century   14th Century   15th Century   Later

NORTH TRANSEPT

TOWER   NAVE   CHANCEL

SOUTH AISLE

PORCH   SOUTH TRANSEPT

0   10
metres

Plan of Mylor Church

Cross at Mylor

North Hill Church

NORTH HILL   *St Torney*   SX 273766

The 14th century chancel has a crocketed ogee-headed niche or Easter Sepulchre in the north wall and ogee-headed niches around the eastern corners inside. Below the north window is a shelf with tiny traceried niches at the back. The rest is late 15th to early 16th century work probably by the same masons that worked at St Neots. There are four bay arcades with slim Cornish standard piers carrying wide arches and original ceiled wagon roofs. The granite south aisle is embattled with pinnacles and has a rib-vaulted porch with an upper room. The west tower has set-back buttresses and an unusual decorative band on the sill of the west window. There is a plain Norman font. The family pew with inlaid woodwork on the doors is of 1724. The monuments include a slate with a skull to Henry Spoure, d1603, an altar tomb with Death and an allegory of the Ascension to Thomas Vincent, d1606 and his wife and family, a slate with three arches to Richard Spoure, d1653, and kneeling figures of Henry Spoure, d1688, with his sister and parents.

NORTH PETHERWIN   *St Paternus*   SX 282896

The north aisle is Norman with a three bay arcade with scalloped capitals to the piers. The double chamfered pointed arches can hardly be earlier than c1200 and the clerestory above with the openings above the piers is probably of c1300. The north doorway is of the same period and has a Victorian porch in front of it. The rest is late medieval and comprises a two bay north chapel twice as wide as the aisle, a south aisle with a five bay arcade and a porch, a chancel projecting one more bay to the east and a west tower with diagonal buttresses, cusped pinnacles and gargoyles below the battlements. The altar rails of the 1680s now lie under the tower arch. Part of the wainscoting of the rood screen survives. There are a few bench ends exhibiting the Instruments of the Passion.

Tower plinth carvings, North Tamerton

NORTH TAMERTON   *St Denis*   SX 302974

The unbuttressed granite tower of three stages with embattled pinnacles has crude carvings on the plinth showing squares with trefoils, quatrefoils, stars, etc, with leaf infillings. The south aisle has granite bands at the level of the window sills and the springing of the window arches. It has an arcade of standard Cornish type. There are a few old bench ends and there is a slate slab to Walter Robins, d1706.

OTTERHAM   *St Denis*   SX 169909

The tower arch has Norman imposts but the rest of the tower seems much later. The church was much restored in 1889, losing a Norman north transept in the process, and now lacks features of interest apart from two fonts, one Norman, damaged, and ornamented with large lozenges and an incised roll round the base.

PADSTOW   *St Petroc*   SW 915754

The chancel east end and the heavily buttressed lower part of the tower are 13th century. The embattled tower top is later. The arcades are of five bays for the nave and two lower bays for the chancel. They are probably 14th century, and the windows of the south chapel are certainly of that period. This chapel has an arch dividing it from the south aisle. The south aisle buttresses have animals and an angel with a shield. Both aisles retain original wagon roofs. The fine octagonal font with demi-figures of angels at the corners and the twelve Apostles in niches in between is 15th century. One bench end shows a fox preaching to geese and the pulpit of c1530 has panels with symbols of the Passion. A brass with a half figure of a priest of 1421 lies on the chancel floor. There is a monument with a cherub stepping onto an old man's shoulder to Sir Nicholas Prideaux, d1627, with life-sized figures of his children, and a more modest monument to Edmund Prideaux, d1693. The churchyard has fine 18th century gates and a Saxon cross shaft with interlaced plaits.

North Tamerton Church

Padstow Church

PAUL   *St Paulinus*   SW 464271

This is quite a large late-medieval church with arcades of nine bays with double-chamfered arches on octagonal piers. The west tower has set-back buttresses and a NW stair turret rising above the pinnacles. There are niches above and either side of the west window. The narrower arch inserted in the seventh arch from the west of the north arcade may have been inserted using older material from elsewhere when the church was repaired after being wrecked during the Spanish raid on Penzance in 1595. Most of the windows have been restored. Part of the inscription on the monument with cherubs and ships to Captain Stephen Hutchens, d1709, is in Cornish. There is also a monument to John Badcock, d1784. An obelisk near the churchyard SE gate was set up by Prince Lucien Bonaparte to commemorate Dolly Pentreath, d1778, the last person who could speak the Cornish language.

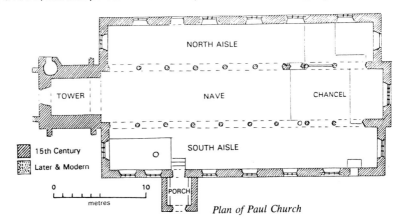

Plan of Paul Church

William Achim, Pelynt

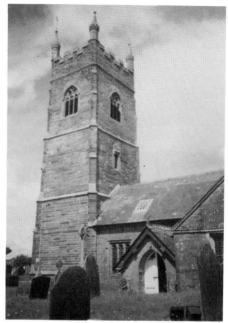

Pelynt Church

PELYNT   *St Nonna or St Mary*   SX 203550

The corner-buttressed west tower with one small ogival-headed window is 14th century. The south transept has 15th century windows like the rest of the church but the masonry must be older. The medieval north arcade was replaced c1680 by an arcade of depressed segmental arches on granite columns of the Tuscan Doric order. The nave has a ceiled wagon roof with old carved bosses. A slate slab shows William Achim, d1589, in armour. There is a tomb chest and a wall-slab with a relief of John Buller of Tregarrick, d1615, with his wife and twelve children. There are other monuments to Edward Trelawny, d1639 and Elizabeth Vyvyan, d1640. The pastoral staff belonged to Sir Jonathan Trelawny, Bishop of Exeter and Winchester, d1721.

PERRANARWORTHAL   *St Piran*   SW 779389

The church is of 1884 by St Aubyn apart from a 15th century tower of granite blocks with pinnacles on angels and a Norman typmanum inside the south doorway with a lamb and cross with an outer leaf-scroll moulding. See front cover picture.

PERRANUTHNOE   *St Piran and St Nicholas*   SW 537296

The unbuttressed west tower of granite blocks is 15th century. The rest of the small church was heavily restored in 1883. The 15th century north aisle has a blocked original doorway, a rood-loft staircase and an arcade of five bays with square piers with four demi-shafts. The south side is earlier, with a south transept of rough masonry with a squint to the rebuilt chancel and a porch with an outer entrance of 13th or 14th century date. The 13th century font has trefoil-headed blank niches. There is a monument to Henry Cole, d1775.

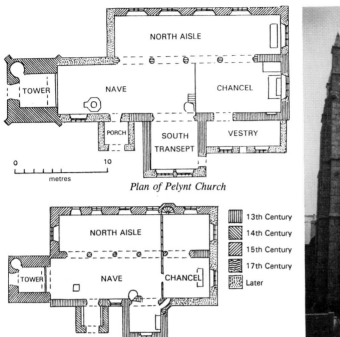

NORTH AISLE

TOWER NAVE CHANCEL

PORCH SOUTH VESTRY
TRANSEPT

0 10
metres

Plan of Pelynt Church

NORTH AISLE

TOWER NAVE CHANCEL

Plan of Perranuthnoe Church

|||| 13th Century

14th Century

15th Century

17th Century

Later

Perranzabuloe Church

PERRANZABULOE   *St Piran*   SW 770520

Except for the tower the church was rebuilt in 1804 and remodelled in 1879. Materials were brought here from the second church of St Piran in the Sands including a an octagonal 15th century font with figures of the Virgin and three Apostles in niches. The west screen incorporates early 16th century bench ends. The slate plate to Perran Hoskyn, d1675 is the best of several monuments of this type. Several medieval window heads are reset in the lychgate.

PHILLACK   *Dedication Unknown*

The rebuilding of 1856 by William White left only the 15th century tower of granite blocks, a font of uncertain date with a rosette, cross, and other motifs in medallions, some 16th century linenfold panelling at the east end, parts of the rood screen now incorporated in the pulpit and a 6th or 7th century stone with an XP monogram in the gable of the south porch. In the churchyard are three other Saxon relics; an inscribed stone, half of a coped stone, and a wheel-cross with a crucifixion and plait-work.

PHILLEIGH   *St Filius*

The octagonal font with two flat blank niches with pointed heads on each side is 13th century and the north transept could also be of that period and the west tower with buttresses low down on the north and south sides is probably not much later. The south aisle with an arcade of nine narrow bays with circular piers with four attached shafts is probably mid to late 14th century, but the vindows are Victorian.

PILLATON   *St Odulph*   SX 367644

The 13th or 14th century north transept is connected to the chancel by a large squint in which is set the rood-loft staircase. The west tower of granite blocks with set-back buttresses is 15th century, as is the south aisle with an arcade of six bays with slim square piers with four attached demi-shafts. There are old wagon-roofs in the transept, aisle and porch. There is a fine monument to James Tillie, d1772.

POLPERRO   *St John the Baptist*   SX 207510

The church was only built in 1838 as a chapel-of-ease to Lansallos but has in the porch a small square bowl with stairs and rosettes which may be Norman.

PORTHILLY   *St Michael*   SW 936754

The small church by an estuary was heavily restored in 1865-7, when the porch-tower was added. The font is Norman and the south transept has a 13th century east lancet. Foundations have been traced of the former north transept. A tiny south chapel was added in the 15th century. The pulpit has early 16th century linenfold panelling and the framework of the rood screen survives. In the churchyard is a wheel-type Saxon cross-head from St Miniver. The stump of the shaft has plait-work.

POUGHILL   *St Olaf*   SS 222078

The south aisle has an arcade of the usual Cornish type in granite. The east bay of this aisle and the north aisle have shorter and thicker sandstone piers of more complex section. Both parts have windows of late 14th century type and there are wagon roofs with bosses. The west tower has set-back buttresses. The 13th century font has two tiers of blank arches with pointed heads. There are bench ends with allegories of the Instruments of Christ's Passion, and Royal Arms of Charles II with strapwork decoration. The south door is medieval.

Philleigh Church

Poundstock Church

POUNDSTOCK *St Neot* SX 202995

The south transept may be Norman. A former north transept was incorporated in a 15th century aisle, the west part of which was built first. The square font with two tiers of blank niches with pointed heads is 13th century. Near it lie a stoup and some old carved stones. The pulpit and a table are Jacobean and there are some old bench ends in the chancel and a chest of c1530-50. On the tower south wall are Royal Arms with strapwork decoration. Faded wall-paintings in the north aisle show the Tree of Deadly Sins, the Warning to the Sabbath-Breakers and the Weighing of Souls.

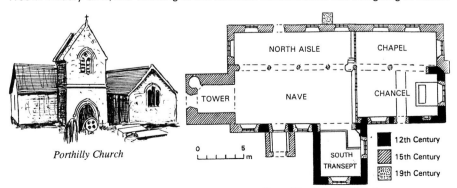

Porthilly Church

NORTH AISLE   CHAPEL

TOWER   NAVE   CHANCEL

SOUTH TRANSEPT

0   5   m

■ 12th Century
▨ 15th Century
▥ 19th Century

Plan of Poundstock Church

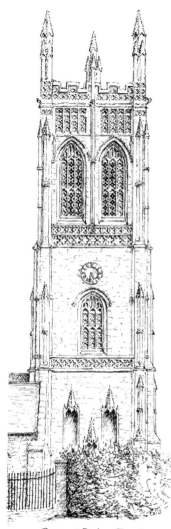

Tower at Probus Church

Chapel on Rame Head

PROBUS   *St Probus and St Grace*   SW 899478

The west tower with set-back buttresses is 37m high, the tallest among those of the Cornish parish churches. It was under construction in 1523, the main patron being John Tregian of Golden. There are quatrefoils on the plinth. A second decorative band has its upper moulding continued over the west doorway. There are three canopied statue niches on each of the north and south sides. Further bands of quatrefoils mark off the second level with three light windows and the third level with similar windows in pairs. Above them are sets of four vertical strips of quatrefoils and then traceried battlements with lofty pinnacles. The whole ensemble is more typical of Somerset than Cornwall. The tower arch is lofty and has panelled responds. The rest of the church is also late medieval with tall arcades of seven bays with more complex mouldings of the piers and arches than usual in Cornwall. The screens of the chancel, north chapel and tower incorporate old bench ends. The monuments include a brass to John Wulvedon, d1514 and his wife, and a seated mourning figure holding a portrait of Thomas Hawkins, d1766, with a flying angel above and pyramid behind.

QUETHIOCK   *St Hugo*   SX 313647

This is an interesting church with much of a cruciform late 13th to early 14th century building preserved. The ends of the two transepts and west wend of the nave have corner buttresses. The south transept is connected to the chancel by a large squint containing the rood-loft staircase. Only the north end of the north transept with an early 14th century tomb recess inside survives projecting slightly from the north wall of an aisle taken through it, with a four bay arcade of standard type. At that time a south porch was added and a thin tower built within the nave west end. On the south side there is a staircase turret rising to battlements at the height where the tower rises above the nave roof. There are fine old wagon-roofs and a few bits of 15th century stained glass remain in one north window. There is a tomb chest with a slate top and back plates to Hugh Halkinow, d1599, and brasses to Roger Kyngdon, d1471, and Richard Chiverton, d1631, with their wives and children.

RAME *St German*

SX 426491 & 418485

The chancel has two 13th century windows and the west tower with lancets, a plain arch towards the nave and a broach-spire with dormer windows must also have formed part of the church consecrated in 1259. Still earlier is the Norman tympanum with three circles with a four-spoked wheel, a four-petalled flower, and saltire crosses. The south aisle has a fine ceiled wagon roof and an arcade of five bays with circular piers with four demi-shafts. A squint connects the north transept and the chancel. There are several old bench ends with tracery. There is a monument to Roger Ashton, Vicar of St Andrew's, Plymouth, d1677.

On Rame head is a small derelict vaulted 14th century chapel.

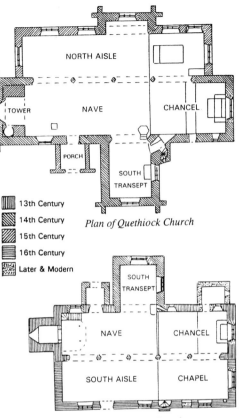

▓	13th Century
▨	14th Century
▨	15th Century
▤	16th Century
▨	Later & Modern

Plan of Quethiock Church

Plan of Rame Church

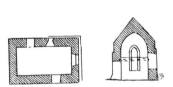

Rame Head Chapel: Plan & section

0   10
metres

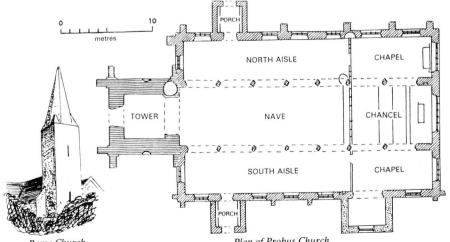

Rame Church

Plan of Probus Church

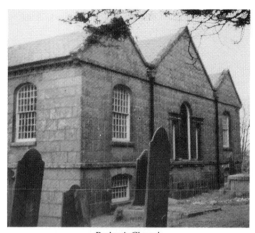

Redruth Church

Roche Chapel

Roche Chapel

Roche Chapel: plan

REDRUTH   *St Euny*   SW 691413

The church is of 1756 with white columns up to the ceiling and a Venetian east window. The only older parts are the 15th century west tower, also of granite, with set-back buttresses and a fine tower arch with panelled jambs, and a demi-figure from a Norman corbel table now fixed on the tower north wall. Excavations have revealed the footings of the Norman church, which had an east apse.

In Cross Street is what was originally the chapel of St Rumon, later a prison, and then in the 1780s and 90s the home of the celebrated inventor William Murdoch.

ROCHE   *St Gonand*   SW 987597 & 991596

The church was rebuilt in 1822 and the south aisle was rebuilt again in 1890 by J.D.Sedding so the only ancient parts are the tall 15th century west tower with set-back buttresses and a circular Norman font with angels' heads at the corners with interlaced serpents between them. In the churchyard is a Saxon cross with incised serpentine lines, irregular holes, and a decorated head.

Spectacularly sited on a granite tor SE of the village is a chapel of St Michael licensed in 1409. The perilous access is by an iron step ladder up the rock, through a doorway into the priest's room below the chapel, out onto the crag the other side, and then round and up to the chapel, of which the east and north walls stand high.

RUAN LANIHORNE *St Rumon*

SW 895420

The low west tower of slate dated 1675 has low corner buttresses. Norman masonry may survive on the south side, where there is a transept. The 15th century added a north aisle with an arcade of six bays with four-centred arches on standard Cornish type granite piers with four capitals and bands of decoration between the capitals and abacus. The square font decorated with quatrefoils and ogival arches is probably 14th century. The pulpit is made from bench ends of c1530. In the south transept is a mutilated effigy of a 13th century priest.

RUAN MAJOR *St Rumon* SW 704165

In the restoration of 1867 the aisles were removed, the arches of the five bay arcades blocked, and the south porch with panelled outer jambs rebuilt against what then became the new south wall. The east end appears to be mostly of that period. The unbuttressed west tower is perhaps 14th century and the arcades later. The church is now an abandoned ruin.

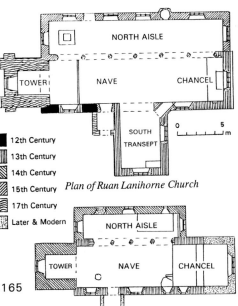

12th Century
13th Century
14th Century
15th Century
17th Century
Later & Modern

Plan of Ruan Lanihorne Church

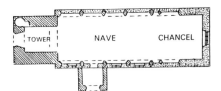

Plan of Ruan Minor Church

Plan of Ruan Major Church

Font at Ruan Lanihorne

The ruined church of Ruan Major

RUAN MINOR   *St Ruan*   SW 721153

This is a small church with an ivy-clad 14th century west tower. The nave and chancel in one are 13th century but the earliest features are 14th century. The north aisle has two windows of that period and a later doorway. It has a four bay arcade with low and narrow arches on piers of Cornish standard type. The small Norman font has a chevron motif upon it.

ST AGNES   *St Agnes*   SW 720507

In the church of 1848 by Piers St Aubyn is a poorbox held up by the figure of a hungry man and a 15th century font decorated with quatrefoils.

ST ALLEN   *St Alleyne*   SW 822506

The tall west tower has set-back buttresses. It is of granite with a top stage of slate and has a high stair turret with a round spire renewed in the 19th century. There is a blocked 13th century north doorway with one order of columns with stiff-leaf on one of the capitals. Of the same period is a lancet in the chancel and perhaps the tower west doorway. The south aisle has a porch and an arcade or four bays with granite piers of the Cornish standard type. There are three crosses in the churchyard.

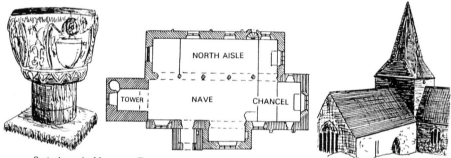

St Anthony-in-Meneage: Font and plan of church

St Anthony-in-Roseland Church

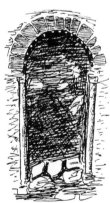

St Allen Church

Norman doorway at St Allen

St Anthony-in-Meneage Church

ST ANTHONY-IN-MENEAGE   *St Dunstan*   SW 783256

The chancel has one south window which may be 13th century. The north aisle is probably late 14th century and has tiny buttresses, a rood-loft staircase and an arcade of five bays with double-chamfered arches on slim octagonal piers. The south doorway is 15th century like the unbuttressed granite west tower with pinnacles on angels and the nave and aisle roofs, but the porch must be earlier and seems to have existed before the shallow south transept was added. The circular font with an inscription and angels bearing shields is probably 15th century.

Interior of St Anthony-in-Meneage Church

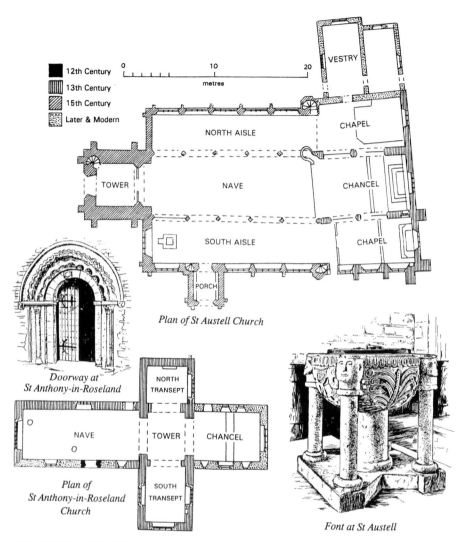

12th Century
13th Century
15th Century
Later & Modern

0   10   20
metres

VESTRY

NORTH AISLE

CHAPEL

TOWER

NAVE

CHANCEL

SOUTH AISLE

CHAPEL

PORCH

Plan of St Austell Church

*Doorway at
St Anthony-in-Roseland*

NORTH
TRANSEPT

NAVE

TOWER

CHANCEL

SOUTH
TRANSEPT

*Plan of
St Anthony-in-Roseland
Church*

Font at St Austell

ST ANTHONY-IN-ROSELAND   *St Anthony*   SW 855320

The church is cruciform with a central tower covered by a timber and lead spire. It served a priory which was a cell of the Augustinian priory at Plympton, there normally being just two canons in residence. The chancel was demolished in 1540 but rebuilt in 1850. Parts of the church are 13th century with foliage capitals on the east and west arches under the tower, and trefoil-headed piscinas in the transepts. The north transept is shorter than its twin and adjoins the house of the Spry family (to whom there are 19th century monuments) between the church and the sea. The nave has been heavily restored but preserves a Norman south doorway with columns with scalloped capitals and crescents with foliage on the voussoirs. The church was repaired in 1338 after an attack by French pirates.

St Austell Church

ST AUSTELL   *Holy Trinity*   SX 014524

The west tower of Somerset type bears the arms of Bishop Courtenay of Exeter (1478-87) and has four apostles in niches on the north, east and south sides, whilst on the west are figures of the Trinity, the Annunciation. There are pinnacles at the top and four strips of ornamentation. The clock face with bosses for the hours is probably 16th century. The south chapel two bay arcade is early 13th century, the north chapel arcade is mid to late 13th century, the pier there being octagonal with attached shafts on the diagonals. The chancel east window and the north aisle east window have intersecting tracery and pointed quatrefoils of about the time when a chantry chapel of St Michael was endowed c1290. The nave has five bay arcades with slender piers of standard Cornish section. Some windows and the wagon roofs survived the heavy restoration in 1872 by G.E.Street. The aisles and the two storey porch with openwork tracery on the outer arch are all-embattled. Also on the porch are angels holding shields, shields with the Instruments of the Passion, Rusurrection, Ascension, and Christ in Glory. The pillar piscina and the font with corner faces, dragons and trees of life are both Norman. Parts of the rood screen remain and a few old bench ends. The oak chest is of 1662. There is an urn to Joseph Sawle, 1769.

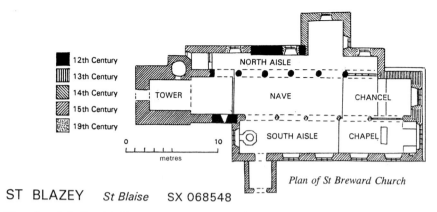

12th Century
13th Century
14th Century
15th Century
19th Century

TOWER

NORTH AISLE

NAVE

CHANCEL

SOUTH AISLE

CHAPEL

0   10

metres

Plan of St Breward Church

ST BLAZEY   *St Blaise*   SX 068548

The church built c1440 was heavily restored by Moffat in 1839, a north aisle being added to match the south aisle with an arcade of standard Cornish type piers with fleur-de-lis crests or battlements on the abaci. The original south porch outer entrance was moved to the south side of the unbuttressed west tower of granite blocks with short pinnacles and an ogivial headed niche with side finials on the middle stage. The goblet-shaped font is of c1600. A slate plate of 1701 depicts Richard Killiowe, d1689, and there is a tablet with columns and angels to Henry Scovell, d1727.

ST BREOCK   *St Breock*   SW 977717

This was a cruciform 13th century church. The nave doorways and the lower parts of the tower with a NE stair turret are 14th century as are one nave window and the east window of the south aisle. The aisle has a six bay arcade of standard Cornish type with four-centred arches and 15th century windows. The font is 15th century. There is a 13th century foliated cross-slab with an inscription and a brass of c1510 to one of the Tredenick family, one of the figures of his two wives being missing. There is also a slate slab to Charles Tredenick, d1578 and a wall monument with kneeling figures of one of the Prideaux-Brune family, d1598, and his wife.

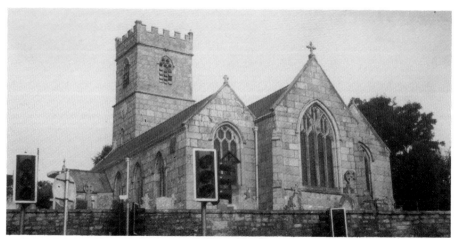

St Blazey Church

ST BREWARD *St Bruerdus*

SX098774

The north arcade of six bays is Norman with circular piers having scalloped capitals, except for one with tree-motifs. The fourth and fifth piers are longer and probably later than the others. The north transept is early too. The rest is late medieval, the tower being unbuttressed at the base but with a later third storey recessed to allow corner buttresses, a south arcade of standard type with flat four-centred arches, windows of four lights and five at the east end, a south porch and an original wagon-roof. The font is made up of Norman parts. The reredos and north chapel screen contain old bench ends. The slate plates by chancel north wall have come from the tomb chest of Christopher Rogers, d1609.

ST BURYAN *St Berian* SW 409258

In 1473 a commission recommended that the 13th century church should be pulled down and rebuilt, so only the lofty tower with set-back buttresses and a NE stair-turret rising above the pinnacles is older than that apart from the chancel east end and a Norman pier in the chancel north wall. There are arcades of four bays for the nave, then a much restored screen and short pieces of wall before there are two further arches on each side to the north and south chapels. The screen has upright motifs in the wainscoting and the rood beam has an upper trail of vine and a lower trail with birds, beasts, grotesque heads half hidden by foliage. There are traces of the red, blue and gold colouring. The font with angels holding shields at three corners is 14th or 15th century. One of the bench ends used in the litany desk is carved with a mermaid. The choir stalls have miserichords or hinged seats with shields. There is a 13th century foliated cross-slab with an inscription to Clarice de Bolleit.

St Buryan Church

Crosshead at St Buryan

ST CLEER   *St Clarus*   SX 247682

The lofty west tower of granite blocks has set-back buttresses and pinnacles in relief below the main pinnacles of the top. The arcades are of four bays with an extra lower bay for the chancel chapels. The north arcade is of c1400 with octagonal piers. The 15th century south arcade has piers and arch mouldings of a more complex form than usual. The windows on this side were also of that date, but the square-headed north windows were later (they are all renewed). A squint connects the north aisle and chancel. Older relics are the Norman north doorway with one order of columns and chevrons on the outer voussoirs and the 13th century font with five flat pointed blank niches on each side. The paintings of bibical verses with 18th century cartouches were probably originally fixed the sprandrels of the arcades. There is a slate depicting Robert Langeford, d1614 and his wife and family all kneeling.

Some distance down a village street to the NE is a vaulted 15th century building containing a holy well. It has piers on the front and sides.

ST CLEMENT   *St Clement*   SW 851439

The stone dated 1326 on the tower is probably not ancient but the tower may well be 14th century. It has buttresses facing north and south only ending in gargoyles at the second stage. The top stage is later. The church was heavily restored in 1865 but the north transept still has 13th century lancets. Its arch towards the nave matches the six bay arcade of Cornish standard piers with finely moulded capitals and arches that are almost semi-circular. The tower screen is made up of parts from the former rood screen. The octagonal font with tracery is 16th century. The earliest monument is of 1796. In the churchyard is a Saxon cross with Latin and Ogham inscriptions.

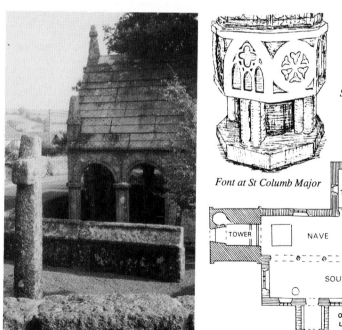

Holy Well at St Cleer

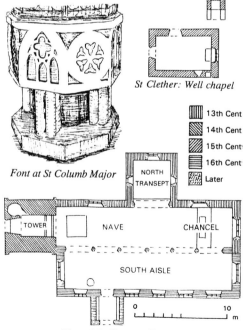

St Clether: Well chapel

▥	13th Cent	
▨	14th Cent	
▧	15th Cent	
▤	16th Cent	
▦	Later	

Font at St Columb Major

NORTH TRANSEPT

TOWER   NAVE   CHANCEL

SOUTH AISLE

0   10
m

Plan of St Clement Church

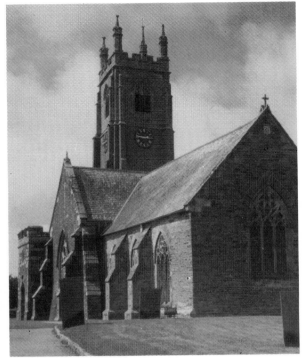

St Clement Church   *St Columb Major Church*

ST CLETHER *St Clederus* SX 205844

The rebuilding of 1865 left only the plain 15th century west tower, a plain Norman font, and three scalloped capitals from a Norman arcade with thick circular piers. Delightfully situated below a cliff above the River Inney some distance south of the church is a 15th century well chapel with a three light east window, a narrow south window and a west doorway. Water from the well outside to the north flows under the chapel east end to come out in a niche in the south wall.

ST COLUMB MAJOR *St Columba* SW 912637

This is an important church in a commanding position. The west tower is of four stages with arches in the north and south sides of the lowest stage and set-back buttresses. The arcades have two-centred arches on square piers with four attached demi-shafts. There are three arches for the nave aisles, then arches for the transepts, and finally more arches for the chancel chapels. They may be as early as c1300, the period of the font with crude faces in quatrefoils and tracery, and the restored south chapel windows are of the Geometrical style of that period with cusped circles and cusped pointed quatrefoils. The south doorway with ballflowers in a hollow on the jambs and voussoirs and heads for label-stops plus the piscinas of the chancel and south chapel are early 14th century. There are 15th century bench ends with shields with initials and the Instruments of the Passion and other motifs. There are brasses of the 1540s and the 1630s to three John Arundels with their wives and children.

Interior of St Columb Major Church

ST COLUMB MINOR   *St Columba*   SW 839624

The granite west tower of four stages has set-back buttresses. The 14th century arcades of six bays with two-centred arches on piers of four major and four minor shafts are much restored but some of the windows are late medieval. The Norman font has five shafts with beasts, interlace, and angels. Two bench ends remain of those made in 1525. There are painted plaster Royal Arms with strapwork decoration.

ST CONSTANTINE'S   *St Constantine*   SW 866747

This ruined chapel comprising a nave and chancel with a south aisle and west tower is thought to date from the 1390s.

ST DENNIS   *St Dennis*   SW 951583

The dedication may refer to the word dinas, a fort, for the church lies within a hillfort 210m above sea level with fine views, the churchyard wall being where the inner rampart was. Only the granite tower with a stair-turret escaped being rebuilt in 1847.

ST DOMINICK   *St Dominica*   SX 399678

The late 13th century west tower has diagonal buttresses, a broad stair turret on the SE and a 16th century corbelled-out top stage. Below the parapet each side has sunk panels containing figures. The 14th century south arcade has double-chamfered arches on square piers with four attached demi-piers. The 15th century north arcade has four hollows on the arches and piers of standard Cornish type. Parts of the roofs are old. On a tomb chest are recumbent effigies of Sir Anthony Rous, d1622 and his son, d1620. A canopy of thirteen marble columns has gone. There is also a monument of 1749 by J.R.Veale to John Clarke.

St Enoder Church

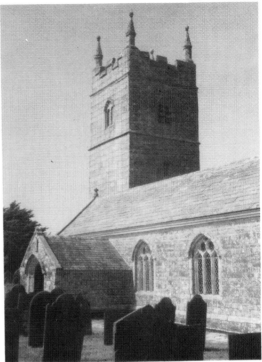

St Endellion Church

ST ENDELLION   *St Endellienta*   SW 997787

There is a quatrefoil pattern on the plinth of the unbuttressed three-stage tower of granite slabs. The 15th century arcades are of five bays with four-centred arches on granite piers of standard Cornish type. Some of the capitals have large horizontal leaves. The aisle windows are of three lights and the east end has a five light window flanked by others of four lights. The roofs were restored in the 1930s and a medieval rafter was then discovered to be dated 1675, presumably referring to repairs. The south doorway has fleurons in the jambs and voussoirs. There are old bench ends and a plain Norman font. The fine tomb chest with deep vaulted side niches in the south aisle is of c1400. The same craftsmen must have also made the stoup by the south doorway with acorns and coats of arms.

ST ENODER   *St Enoder*   SW 892570

The south arcade of four bays with octagonal piers is 14th century. Of the 15th century are the embattled south porch of granite with demi-figures of angels and quatrefoils on the plinths, the north arcade of seven bays with piers of Cornish stadard type, the three eastern bays lower than the rest, and the north transept. The date 1711 on the north side refers to repairs made after the original tower collapsed in 1684 and damaged that side. The tower then built has Baroque scrolls instead of set-offs on the buttresses. There are old bench ends with shields, a Norman font with corner faces and a criss-cross pattern, a fragment of 15th century stained glass in the SE window, and a slate plate with kneeling figures to Dorothy Tanner, d1634.

ST ENODOC   *St Enodoc*   SW 931772

This chapel was dug out of the sands and restored in 1863. It now lies among golf links. The nave and the north transept with the lowest stage of the tower north of the transept are Norman. The tower upper stage with a tiny spire is 13th century. In the 14th or 15th century a south chapel was added with a three bay arcade of the usual Cornish type. In the churchyard is a tomb with incised crude effigies of John Mably and daughter, 1687. It is said to be the most recent of its type in England.

ST ERME   *St Hermes*   SW 847499

The rebuilding of 1819-20 by John Foulston left the broad west tower of three stages with set-back buttresses, the six bay north arcade with semi-circular arches on piers of standard Cornish type, the embattled south porch, a few of the original roof beams, a circular Norman font with a large foliage scroll above four trees of life and a reset brass of 1596 to the Trencreek family.

ST ERNEY   *St Terminus*   SX 371590

The old features comprise a low slate west tower with thick buttresses, a 15th century north aisle with an arcade of four bays with granite piers of the Cornish standard type, and an ancient font with a square bowl with elementary motifs.

St Erney Church

Porch at St Erme

ST ERTH   *St Ercus*   SW 550350

This late 14th century church was heavily restored in 1874, much of the aisles being rebuilt and dormer windows put into the roofs. Their east windows are original, as are the buttressed porch with panelled jambs to the outer entrance, the six bay arcades and the unbuttressed west tower with grotesque heads below the battlements. The south arcade and western part of the north arcade are of the usual Cornish type but the eastern part of the north arcade has taller piers and moulded capitals with leaves on the abaci. There are two saltire crosses on each side of the square Norman font. There are painted Royal Arms. In the churchyard are a crosshead and a Saxon cross-shaft with a crucifix and interlace. There is a late medieval lantern cross in the middle of the village.

ST ERVAN   *St Hermes*   SW 892703

This is a rare instance in Cornwall of a 13th century cruciform church never enlarged by later aisles. The chancel is narrower than the nave and inclines to the south. Two north windows and the south doorway are 15th century and the only 13th century opening is the north doorway. The arches to the transepts and chancel plus many windows are Victorian. The upper part of the 15th century tower was rebuilt of reinforced concrete in 1955. There are ten slate memorial plates scattered around the inside of the church.

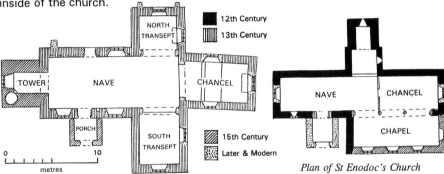

Plan of St Ervan Church

Plan of St Enodoc's Church

St Enodoc's Church

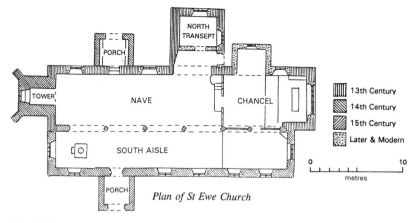

Plan of St Ewe Church

ST EVAL   *St Uvelus*   SW 872692

The church lies alone almost surrounded by a military airfield. The tower was rebuilt at the expense of Bristol merchants in 1724-7 as it formed a useful landmark for their ships. The nave north wall is Norman with one original window. The south aisle with a seven bay arcade with Cornish standard piers with leaves on the abaci is 15th century. The sixth bay east of the base of the former rood screen has a lower arch than the rest. The north transept has an arcade matching that opposite. The cup-shaped font is Norman. There are 15th century bench ends with initials, pairs of shields and Instruments of the Passion. There are also bench backs with arcading and set of Royal Arms. The pulpit is of 1638. The porch is dated 1724 below a sundial.

St Gennys Church

Screen dado, St Eval

Interior of St Eval Church

ST EWE   *All Saints*   SW 978461

The north transept has a 13th century arch towards the nave. The 14th century west tower has diagonal buttresses and an octagonal spire with small broaches, windows at its foot and a band of quatrefoils halfway up. The south aisle of c1390-1400 has a six bay arcade with four-centred arches on piers with four major and four minor shafts with flowers on the capitals and embattled abaci. The Norman font has five supports and four corner faces. The fine rood screen has an elaborate cornice carved with beasts, birds and a naked boy among foliage. The earliest and best of several monuments is that with a bust of William Mohun, d1737, and broken pediments.

ST GENNYS   *St Gennys*   SX 149972

The two lower stages of the west tower facing the sea are of c1200. Original are the small windows and the pointed arch on simple imposts towards the nave. The top was added by E.Sedding early in the 20th century. Norman masonry also survives in the chancel east end and there is also a Norman font with several blank niches with pointed heads on each side of the square bowl. There are arcades of four bays of low arches, three on the north side with complex mouldings and Cornish standard piers with flower motifs on the capitals, whilst the rest has double-chamfered four-centred arches on octagonal granite piers. Old bench ends are made into a litany desk.

ST GERMANS   *St Germanus*   SX 359578

Nothing remains of the Saxon cathedral here, bishops being recorded from 931 until the 1040s. The bishopric became part of the new diocese of Exeter in 1050. Bishop Bartholomew had the church rebuilt in the 1160s and 70s to serve an Augustinian priory. Nothing remains of the eastern end of his church but the western part remains the most spectacular Norman work amongst Cornish parish churches. It has a central west portal of seven orders with many chevrons. Flanking it are two towers with broad clasping pilaster buttresses and pointed arches with roll-mouldings towards the nave. An upper gallery over the west portal connected the second storey of the towers, there being here three windows with nook-shafts lighting the nave. Above this level the north tower is octagonal, whilst the south tower remains square with a mixture of Norman and late medieval windows. Just two bays of arches of differing widths remain on the south side of the former Norman aisles. The circular piers with square scalloped capitals support pointed arches of two orders, above which are remains of the original clerestory windows with a profusion of chevrons.

The chancel consecrated in 1261 extended 17m beyond the present east wall until it collapsed in 1592. Four arches of that period connect the Norman part of the arcade to the new east wall in which is reset a five-light 15th century window. The embattled south aisle bearing the arms of Bishop Lacy (1420-50) is 2m wider than the nave for four bays with four-light windows, then there is a 14th century south chapel with two three-light windows in the east wall with a niche between them and a huge six-light window facing south. The aisle has a 15th century west porch adjoining the south wall of the south tower. It is vaulted and has openings both to the west and south. The north side is no longer aisled and has no work older than the transeptal projection of 1803 to contain the pew of the Earls of St Germans, who lived in the adjoining house of Port Eliot on the site of the former cloistral buildings. The transept arch contains reused Norman parts. East of it is a 19th century vestry.

Elliot Church, St. Germans.

West front, St Germans Church

Interior of St Germans Church

There is a damaged Purbeck marble font of c1200. One late 14th century choir stall has a miserichord depicting a man called Dando punished for hunting on Sunday. The only pre-19th century monuments are a tomb chest of John Moyle, d1661, in the vestry and a fine composition of 1722 by Rysbrack with Edward Eliot reclining on a sarcophagus with a mourning figure on one side, a pyramid in relief and putti.

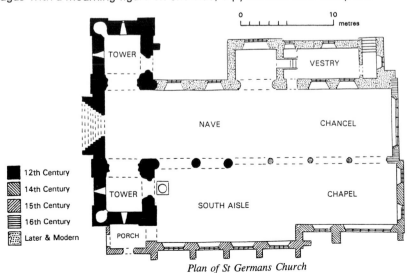

Plan of St Germans Church

St Gluvias Church

ST GLUVIAS *St Gluviacus* SW 787346

This, the parish church of Penryn, was rebuilt in 1883 by J.P.St Aubyn except for the west tower of granite blocks with corner buttresses and a NW stair-turret. The monuments include a brass of c1485 to Thomas Killigrew and two wives, wall-monuments to William Pendarves, d1671, and Samuel Pendarves, d1693, with their wives, plus a bust of J.Kempe, d1711, wearing a wig.

ST HILARY   *St Hilary*   SW 550553

The rebuilding of 1854 by William White has left only the 13th century west tower
with broad corner-buttresses and a broach spire. There is a Flemish painting of c1500 with Christ in the act of blessing. An inscribed milestone of c306 in the church has an inscription referring to Constantine the Great. Another stone outside in the churchyard is a 6th or 7th century monument to Notus, son of Notus.

St Issey Church

West doorway at St Germans

ST ISSEY   *St Ida*   SW 928718

The church has been heavily restored, the tower having fallen in 1869. The aisles now have lean-to roofs, not a common sight in Cornwall. The NW vestry is an addition of the 1990s. The 14th century three bay north arcade has piers with four major and four minor shafts. The south arcade is 15th century and has three bays, plus two lower ones for a south chapel. The arches are four-centred and lie on Cornish standard piers with horizontal leaves on the capitals. The reredos has panels with deep niches and little figures probably from the tomb of Lady Matilda Chyverston. In 1399 an indulgence was granted to those visiting the tomb. The font has five supports and motifs such as a cross, star and a candelabra.

ST IVE   *St Ive*

Of the church consecrated in 1338 there remain the north transept and chancel, connected by a squint and both with corner buttresses, and the nave north wall with a blocked doorway and a pair of two-light windows. The transept has three-light windows with pointed trefoils and quatrefoils in the tracery. The east window of five lights is one of the best of its period in Cornwall. The internal jambs have niches with bowed ogival arches with much crocketing. The fragment of a figure of St Christopher may have come from one of these niches. Triple sedilia and a piscina also survive. The lower part of the west tower with set-back buttresses may also be 14th century. The upper part with twelve pinnacles is late 15th or early 16th century, as are the south aisle with a five bay arcade of four-centred arches on piers of standard Cornish type and the diagonally buttressed south porch. The nave, aisle, and porch have original wagon-roofs. The pulpit is dated 1700 but looks a century older. There are Royal Arms of Charles II from 1660 with strapwork ornament.

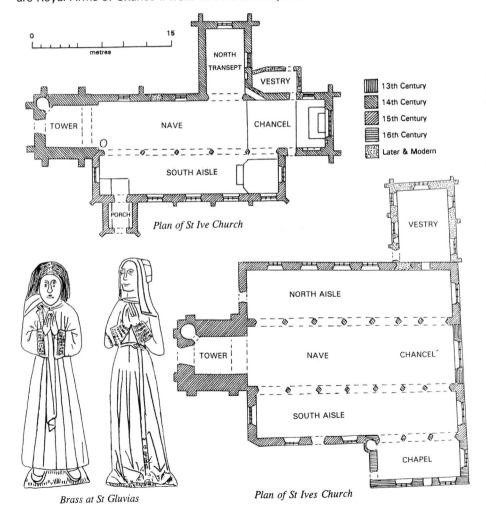

Plan of St Ive Church

Brass at St Gluvias

Plan of St Ives Church

Interior of St Ives Church

ST IVES   *St Ia*   SW 518405

The church was erected in 1410-34 as a chapel-of-ease to Lelant and only attained full parochial status in 1826. It consists of a granite west tower with set back buttresses and corbelled-out pinnacles and a nave and aisles of equal width and height divided by arcades of seven bays of four-centred arches on sandstone piers having demi-shafts connected by a concave-convex-concave pattern. A three bay outer chapel added by the Trenwith family c1500 to the east end of the south side now forms a Lady Chapel. This part has a corbel table with heads. All four east windows are of three lights. The stair in the chapel NW corner gave access to the rood-loft.

There are many old bench ends mostly with pairs of shields and others have been used in the pulpit. Those in the chancel include some profile portraits and have angel shield-bearers instead of poppy-heads. The granite font with a circular bowl with angels with shields on five supports with lions on the bases is probably 15th century. There is a brass of 1463 to one of the Trenwith family with a small figure of St Michael on one side. There is a slate slab of 1642 to the Sise family. In the churchyard is a 15th century cross on an octagonal shaft.

ST JOHN   *St John*   SX 408537

The upper stage of the Norman pyramidal-roofed west tower is recessed. There are original windows on the north and south and a narrow arch towards the nave. The rest of the church is of little interest apart from fragments of old stained glass in one north window.

St Juliot Church

Cross at St Ives

ST JULIOT *St Julitta* SX 129913

The church was restored by Thomas Hardy (the famed novelist) in 1871-2, whose drawings of it are framed inside. He rebuilt the tower at the west end of the granite north aisle and the aisle north wall. The aisle extends one bay beside the chancel and has the usual Cornish type of arcade piers. The square granite font and the embattled south porch with a vault with one transverse arch are 15th century. There is a small bronze relief of the Deposition of Christ made in Italy in the 16th century. In the churchyard are two Saxon crosses, one with the cross arms formed of triangles.

ST JUST-IN-PENWITH *St Just* SW 372315

This is a large late medieval church of granite blocks with an unbuttresssed west tower of three stages and a buttressed porch with battlements and pinnacles. There are two alternating designs of windows and six bay arcades with piers like those at St Ives with capitals with horizontal leaves and fruit. The aisle east windows have tracery of a "palm-tree" pattern. In the north aisle are restored wall paintings of St George and the Warning to to the Sabbath-Breakers, and also an inscribed 5th-6th century stone with an XP monogram.

Interior of St Just-in-Penwith Church

ST JUST-IN-ROSELAND   *St Just*   SW 848358

The church lies in a wooded comb beside a creek off Carrick Sound. The 14th century west tower has diagonal buttresses and a polygonal SE stair-turret rising above the pinnacles. Of the church consecrated in 1261 there survive the north and east walls including the piscina, and a shallow north transept with later windows. The transept now contains the organ and a vestry has been added on the east. Of the 15th century are the font with quatrefoil panels and the south aisle with a six bay arcade of almost semi-circular arches on granite piers of Cornish standard type, plus the south porch with a doorway with openwork tracery now broken off. There is a brass of a priest of c1520.

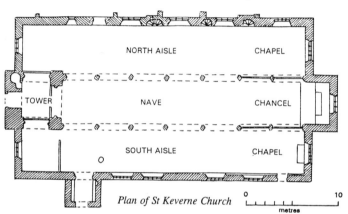

Plan of St Keverne Church

Brass at St Just

St Keverne Church

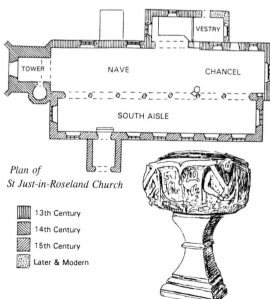

Plan of St Just-in-Roseland Church

▦ 13th Century
▧ 14th Century
▨ 15th Century
▩ Later & Modern

Font at St Keverne Church

ST KEVERNE *St Akeveranus* SW 791213

The church lies by a square and has an octagonal ribbed spire renewed in 1770 because it was a useful landmark. The unbuttresssed tower is flanked by the aisles. There are arcades of seven bays with piers of various sections, those in the nave being more massive than usual, evidently late 13th or 14th century material reused in the 15th century, the period of the windows. On the north wall is a faded wall painting of St Christopher surrounded by scenes of his life. The three staircases in this wall plus the join in the south wall suggest the church was extended eastwards in two stages. The south doorway has suspended shields at capital level. The font is also 15th century and has angels at the corners with shields and inscriptions between them. There are a few old bench ends and the pulpit is Jacobean.

ST KEW *St James* SX 022769

The west tower has set-back buttresses and a rectangular stair-turret rising above the battlements. There are five bay arcades of four-centred arches on granite piers of Cornish standard type. There are three light side windows and others of four and five lights facing east. A north window has stained glass dated 1469 with arms of Henry VI, the Beare, Kingdon and Carminow families. Three rows of four scenes show the story of Christ's Passion from the Entry into Jerusalem to the Harrowing of Hell. A south window contains fragments of a Tree of Jesse and there are fragments of old glass in other windows. Also 15th century are the ceiled wagon-roofs with angels against the wall-plates, the octagonal font with quatrefoil panels, the south door and a crosshead brought in from outside. There are stocks in the porch and a 6th or 7th century stone with inscriptions in Ogham and Latin. There are Royal Arms of 1661.

St Just-in-Roseland Church

St Kew Church

St Mabyn Church

ST KEYNE   *St Keyne*   SX 242608

The south transept may be 13th century and there are two reset 14th century windows in the 15th century north aisle. The west tower may also be 14th century. The plain octagonal font is 15th century.

ST LEVAN   *St Levan*   SW 380222

The 13th century north transept has an original west lancet. The blocked north doorway adjoins it since the nave is quite short. The unbuttressed west tower is late 14th or early 15th century. The transept was given a two bay arcade in the 15th century when an aisle with a six bay arcade of double-chamfered arches on octagonal piers was added on the south side. The aisle has renewed windows and a staircase to the loft over the screen of which the base survives with initials, symbols of the Passion and foliage with two dragons. There are bench ends of the 1530s with pairs of creatures such as fishes, eagles and jesters. The large circular Norman font has a cable moulded lower border, an upper border of saltire crosses, and stairs in circles on the sides. The pulpit of 1752 has some inlay work.

ST MABYN   *St Mabena*   SX 043732

The unbuttressed west tower of three stages with a polygonal NE stair turret not rising the full height may be 14th century, and the square font with shallow blank niches with pointed heads is Norman. The rest is 15th century with seven bay arcades of two-centred arches on piers of Cornish standard type, the arches being narrower in the chancel than they are in the nave. There are three-light side windows and the east end has a five-light window flanked by chapel windows of four lights. There are original ceiled wagon roofs and a few fragments of stained glass.

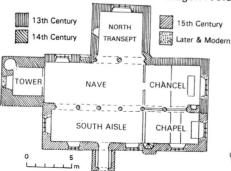

Plan of St Levan Church

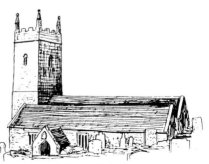

St Levan Church

St Martin-by-Looe Church

ST MARTIN-BY-LOOE   *St Keyne and St Martin*   SX 260550

Much of the church is 15th century with ceiled wagon-roofs and a south aisle of three bays to the nave and a south chapel of two bays to the chancel, with a variety of pier and capital types. Of the church which was dedicated in 1258 there remain a Norman north doorway of four orders with chevrons and a tiny 13th century lancet discovered near the west end of the south wall. The lower two stages of the diagonally buttressed west tower with a SE staircase turret is 14th century. The Norman font has a tree of life and groups of four-petalled flowers. Of the early 17th century are the altar rails and the parclose screen. As well as many early 19th century monuments there are a tomb chest with a flat relief of Philip Mayowe, d1590, and painted kneeling figures of Walter Langdon and his wife, d1667.

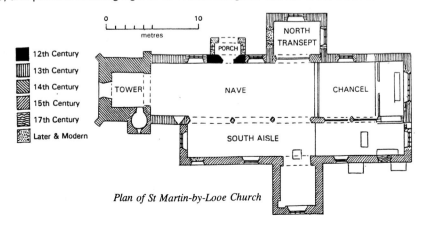

Plan of St Martin-by-Looe Church

ST MARTIN-IN-MENEAGE   *St Martin*   SW 735236

The church is of 1830 and the only old features are the 15th century unbuttressed west tower with heads projecting from the top cornice and a Norman font with corner shafts and rosettes in flat relief.

ST MELLION   *St Mellanus*   SX 389656

The west tower of granite blocks has thin corner buttresses. The church has two 14th century piscinas and renewed windows of that period in the chancel south wall. The late 15th century north aisle has an arcade with piers of standard Cornish section. Two 15th century windows are reused in the modern NE vestry. The pulpit is Jacobean. The earliest of the many monuments of the Coryton family is a brass to Peter, d1551 with his wife and twenty-four children. There are kneeling figures of William, d1651, and William, d1711, with their wives, both with double columns and a coffer-vaulted arch above them. The early 18th century is a remarkably late date for a monument of an essentially Elizabethan and Jacobean type.

ST MERRYN   *St Merryn*   SW 886742

Parts of the nave and chancel are Norman. The north transept with an east lancet is a 13th century addition. Of the 15th century are the south aisle with a seven bay arcade of four-centred arches on piers of standard Cornish type and a wagon roof and windows of three lights. The 15th century octagonal font has demi-figures of angels at the corners and Apostles niches in between. By the same craftsman are three angel corbels, one in the church, the others by the churchyard gates. There are stocks in the porch and Royal Arms of plaster with strapwork decoration. There is a monument with seven kneeling figures of John Michell, d1617 and his family.

St Merryn Church

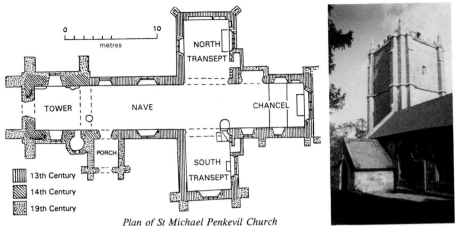

Plan of St Michael Penkevil Church

St Mewan Church

ST MEWAN   *St Mewan*   SW 998519

Norman are two windows in the chancel, part of a font bowl, and the base upon which is set the octagonal 14th century font with tracery panels. There is a south aisle with a five bay arcade and a three bay north chapel. The west tower with set-back buttresses was left unfinished after the second stages had been built.

ST MICHAEL CAERHAYS   *St Michael*   SW 964421

The north side has an early transept and a doorway with a Norman tympanum with a lamb and cross. There is a plain west tower, 14th or 15th century, and a south aisle with an arcade of just two bays with a pier of standard Cornish section, the responds having big horizontal leaves on their capitals. The chancel has a 14th century piscina with crocketed finials and a 15th century angel with a shield. In the aisle are a helmet and swords of the 15th century. The oldest of the monuments is that of 1769 with three urns and drapery to William Trevanion.

ST MICHAEL PENKEVIL   *St Michael*   SW 858423

On the north side of the chancel is a stone recording the dedication of the church in 1261. Transepts were added soon after with tomb niches and sedilia with cinquefoil heads with hoodmoulds with heads for label-stops. The south transept contains a reredos of c1300. Another with flamboyant details in the north transept is 15th century. There are tiny cells behind both of these. The church was repaired in 1319 by Sir John de Trejagu, who founded four chantries in it, the priests serving these living together in a college. Unfortunately the church was very heavily restored in 1863-5 by G.E.Street, many of the features being re-tooled or renewed.

   The collection of monuments starts with two 13th century foliated cross-slabs. There are brasses to John Trenowith, d1497, and the priest John Trembras, d1515, shown in academic robes. There are other brasses to Edward Boscawen, d1619 and his wife, Mary Boscawen, d1622, widow of Peter Coffin, and John Boscawen, 1634. There is a reclining effigy of Hugh Boscawen, d1659, and a bust of Admiral Boscawen, 1763. By Nollekens are monuments to later Boscawens: Edward Hugh, d1774, Frances, d1774, and Elizabeth Ann, Viscountess of Falmouth, d1783.

ST MINVER   *St Menefreda*   SW 964771

The west tower with a rebuilt octagonal broach-spire and the narrow north aisle with an arcade of double-chamfered arches on short octagonal piers are both 13th century. The south aisle with a seven bay arcade of two-centred arches on granite piers of Cornish standard type may be 14th century. Of the 15th century are the wagon roof in the south porch, the octagonal font with traceried panels, and part of the rood screen now set into the tower arch. There are several fine bench ends of the 1530s. The altar rail is 17th century. A scalloped Norman capital discovered in 1927 lies against the west wall. There is a small brass depicting Roger Opy, d1517 and a kneeling figure in profile of John Roe, d1657.

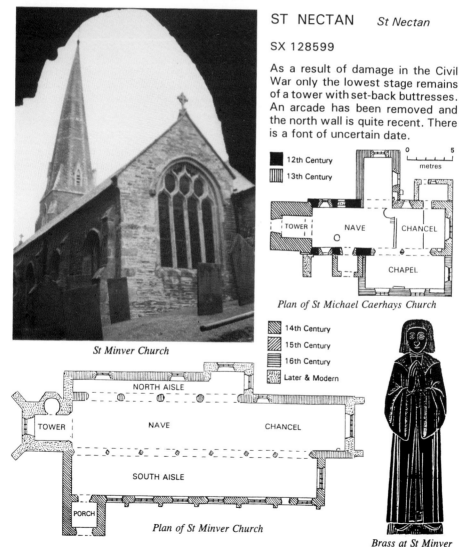

ST NECTAN   *St Nectan*

SX 128599

As a result of damage in the Civil War only the lowest stage remains of a tower with set-back buttresses. An arcade has been removed and the north wall is quite recent. There is a font of uncertain date.

■ 12th Century

▨ 13th Century

Plan of St Michael Caerhays Church

▨ 14th Century

▨ 15th Century

≡ 16th Century

▨ Later & Modern

St Minver Church

Plan of St Minver Church

Brass at St Minver

ST NEOT   *St Anietus*   SX 186679

St Nectan Church

The 14th century west tower has diagonal buttresses and a pointed tunnel-vault with transverse arches. The ogee-headed recess in the chancel is also 14th century. Of the early 15th century are the embattled south aisle and porch forming a show front to impress those coming up the valley. The porch has a tunnel-vault with ribs and five bosses, one of which has four faces, and there is an upper room above. The aisle has a wagon-roof with shield-bearing angels along the wall-plate and the windows are of four lights apart from the east window of five lights. The north aisle has early 16th century windows and has a squint into the chancel. The windows contain an unusually complete set of late-medieval stained glass with many saints and biblical scenes. One window on the north is called the Wives Window since it was donated by wives from the west part of the parish in 1523. The north aisle west window has the Legend of St George, whilst a window on the south shows the story of Noah. The arcades are of seven bays although the east bay on the north side is only half the normal width. The arches are four-centred and lie on piers of Cornish standard type. The 15th century font bowl lies on a 13th century shaft. There are kneeling figures of William Bere, 1610 and his family. In the churchyard is a 10th century cross-shaft with elaborate interlace.

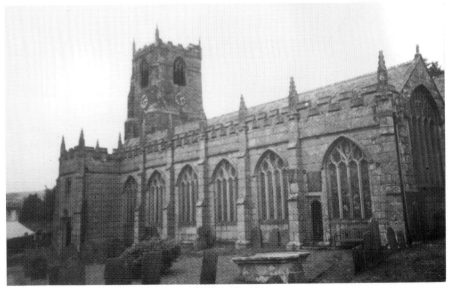

St Neot Church

Tower at St Stephen-by-Launceston

ST NEWLYN EAST   *St Newlina*

SW 828564

The chancel and north transept have Norman masonry and there is a font of that period with angel faces at the corners and intertwined floriated scrolls above lilies in between. Of the 14th century are the niorth doorway and the south chapel with an original piscina. It has an arcade of two lower arches at the end of the six bay arcade of Cornish standard type for the 15th century south aisle. The transept has two arches matching the arcade. The embattled south porch was intended to have an upper room. The set-back buttresses of the 15th century west tower stop at the second of three stages. Eight of the many carved bench ends have beasts. There are plaster Royal Arms with strapwork decoration. There is a bust of Lady Margaret Arundell, d1691 in an open segmental pediment.

ST PINNOCK   *St Pynnochus*   SX 200632

The church comprises a west tower with a polygonal NE stair-turret, a nave with south porch and south transept, and a north aisle with a granite arcade of foy baus of standard Cornish type. The wagon roofs are partly old. The Norman font has corner heads and arms supporting the wide square top.

ST PIRAN'S   *St Piran*   SW 773565

The 6th or 7th century oratory of St Piran was abandoned in the 11th century because it had become engulfed by dunes. It has been excavated and is now sheltered within a building. The walls are bonded with clay and have a seat all round the inside. There is just one unsplayed window on the south side.

The new 11th century church eventually became a long narrow building with transepts, a south aisle added in 1462 and a west tower. It too was engulfed by sands and only footings of it survive, marked by a nearby cross, probably that mentioned in 960. In 1804 a new church of St Piran was built at Lambourne.

Font at St Newlyn East

ST STEPHEN-BY-LAUNCESTON *St Stephen*

SX 324858

Nothing in the church can be associated with the consecration of 1259. The Norman north transept has traces of round arches from former windows. Also Norman are the font and the figures of a seated Christ and a Virgin and Child set on the east wall. There is a north chapel east of this transept. The 14th century south aisle has an arcade of four bays with double-chamfered arches on square piers with four attached demi-shafts. The early 16th century tower of big granite blocks has set-back buttresses with pinacles in relief at the top. There is an incised cross-slab of 1528 and there are slate slabs of 1631 and 1675.

ST STEPHEN-BY-SALTASH *St Stephen*

SX 416584

Until 1881 this was the parish church of Saltash. The tower lies north of the nave west end with a later aisle east of it. There are set-back buttresses and a stair-turret rising as high as the pinnacles but the lowest stage may be 12th century work. The rest is 15th century but not of one period as joints show the chancel was built before the aisles, which in turn are of different dates. Both arcades have piers of the Cornish standard type but differences in the capitals and the arch mouldings show that the north side was built first. There are large windows and ceiled wagon roofs, plus another such roof on the shallow porch with diagonal buttresses and decorated jambs. The large Norman font on five supports has busts at the corners and trees of life and animals on the sides. In a flat niche is a semi-reclining effigy of a lady of c1600-20. There are monuments reset around a corner of W.Hitchens and his wife and their daughter, wife of G.Wadham, d1606.

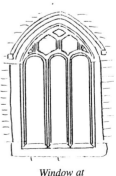

St Stephen-by-Saltash

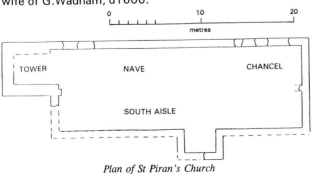

Plan of St Piran's Church

Window at
St Stephen-in-Brannel

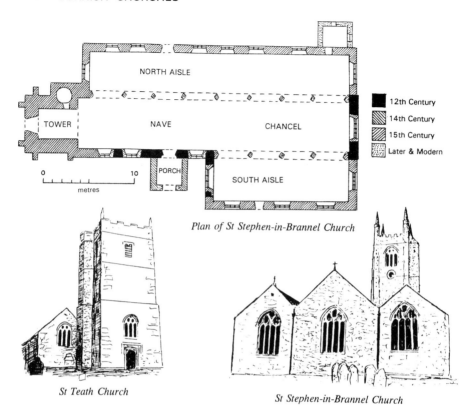

Plan of St Stephen-in-Brannel Church

12th Century
14th Century
15th Century
Later & Modern

NORTH AISLE

TOWER

NAVE

CHANCEL

PORCH

SOUTH AISLE

0   10

metres

St Teath Church

St Stephen-in-Brannel Church

ST STEPHEN-IN-BRANNEL   *St Stephen*   SW 944533

The church is essentially 15th century building of granite with large windows of that period and arcades of eight bays with Cornish standard piers and a west tower with set-back buttresses. The south aisle is known to date from the 1420s. It has a reset Norman doorway with knobs on the voussoirs. Also Norman is the font on five supports with demi-figures at the corners and animals and trees of life between them. The altar rail is early 17th century.

ST TEATH   *St Tetha Virgin*   SX 064806

The first blocked arch of the north arcade and the west respond of the south arcade are Norman, as are the two capitals supporting the north aisle altar. The tower has a polygonal stair turret. The ceiled wagon-roofed 15th century aisles have six bays arcades of four-centred arches on granite piers of Cornish standard type. The south aisle east window is of five lights. The other windows are of three lights, two on the north side having ogival-headed niches for images. Some of the south windows have fragments of original stained glass. The pulpit with the Carminnow family arms is dated 1630 and of about the same period are the panels in the choir stalls and the almsbox. There are bench ends with shields in the aisles. There is a damaged effigy of a 14th century priest with his head flanked by angels. In the churchyard is a restored Saxon cross with leaf scrolls and defaced interlace.

ST TUDY   *St Tudius*   SX 066764

The only pre-15th century features are the Saxon coped stone with blind arcading, interlaced cable, and foliage scrolls, the square Norman font with blank niches in two tiers on one side, and a crudely carved figure from a Norman corbel table which was found in 1932. The tall west tower is unbuttressed. The south aisle is six bays long, the north aisle only three, both having original wagon roofs and four-light east windows in one of which are fragments of old glass, whilst the chancel has a five-light east window. The side windows are of three lights. The arcades of granite have Cornish standard type piers. The late 16th century painting of the Last Supper is Flemish. There are slates with kneeling figures to men who died in 1564 and 1597 with their wives and children, plus others of similar type, and there are life-size kneeling effigies of Anthony Nicholls, d1659.

ST VEEP   *St Vepus*   SX 140550

The west tower with corner buttresses and the south aisle with an arcade of steeply pointed arches on piers with four demi-shafts and four keeled minor shafts with moulded capitals may go back back to the dedication recorded in 1336. The 15th century north aisle has a squint and an arcade with similar piers but without keeling but with horizontal leaves on the capitals. Also of that period are the wall-plates of the wagon-roofs, the porch, the font and most of the restored windows. The 19th century pulpit has thick 17th century brackets attached to it. A few old bench ends remain and a set of Royal Arms. There is a slate plate to Nicholas Courtenay, d1589.

St Tudy Church

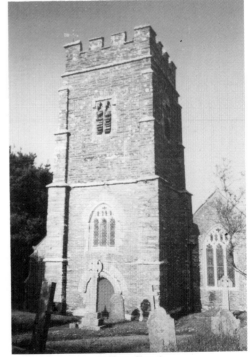

St Veep Church

ST WENN   *St Wenna*   SW 967649

This is a 15th century church, the only older feature being a Norman font with five supports and corner faces plus other motifs. There are aisles with three bay arcades of four-centred arches on piers of four thick and four thinner attached shafts with horizontal leaves on the capitals. The granite west tower has quatrefoils on the plinth and was originally of three stages but now only has two.

ST WINNOW   *St Winnow*   SX 115570

The church lies by the River Fowey with just the vicarage and a farm for company. The north transept has a 13th century arch towards the nave. On the south side is a 15th century aisle with a six bay arcade of the standard Cornish type. The west tower has set-back buttresses. There are old wagon-roofs. The 15th century font of granite has angels with outstretched hands. Some bench ends are 15th century, others are dated 1520, 1590 and 1620. Motifs on them include a St Catherine's Wheel and a man drinking. Several windows retain original stained glass. The fine screen was restored in 1907 by E.H.Sedding. There is a Jacobean altar table and a 17th century pulpit on short bulbous legs. There is a slate to William Sawle, d1651.

Font at St Winnow Church

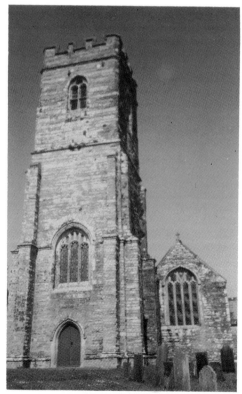

St Winnow Church

Saltash Church

SALTASH   *St Nicholas*   SX 431588

The church ranked only as a chapel-of-ease until 1881. The nave, chancel with two original windows, the south transept, and the north tower beyond a north aisle but originally beyond a north transept are all Norman. A blocked doorway of that period remains on the south side and the font with corner and centre ribs may also be Norman. The squint connecting the south transept and chancel must be later. The north aisle with a five bay arcade of standard Cornish type is 15th century. Both the aisle and nave have wagon-roofs of that period. The north chapel is 14th century, its arcade having double-chamfered arches. A plaque in the north chapel refers to repairs being made to the church in 1589. There are portrait medallions of three naval officers of the Drew family drowned in shipwrecks in 1798 and 1799.

Norman doorway, Saltash

SANCREED   *St Sancredus*   SW 420294

The 13th century north transept has renewed lancets and a two bay arcade inserted when the south aisle was added in the 15th century. The aisle has a porch and a five bay granite arch of standard Cornish type. At the same time a five-light window was inserted in the east wall of the 13th century chancel. The crudely formed and blocked north doorway may be Norman. The unbuttressed west tower with a NE stair-turret is 14th century. The granite font with angels holding shields is 15th century. Panels remaining from the rood screen have interesting carved motifs such as a jester blowing a trumpet with a snake winding up it, a goat among thistles, an owl and the signum tricipit. In the churchyard are two fine Saxon crosses with Crucifixion scenes. One has fine interlace with a biting beast whilst the other has the unusual motif of a lily in a vase. Some distance west of the church, in trees near the Grumble road, are remains of a baptistry and holy well.

Tower, Saltash

SENNEN   *St Sennen*   SW 356255

This is the westernmost church on the English mainland. The reconsecration recorded in 1440 probably refers to the addition of the south aisle with a five bay arcade of four-centred arches on square piers with four attached demi-shafts. The unbuttressed west tower may be late 14th century. The north side has a 13th century transept with a restored lancet and a 15th century arch towards the nave, a blocked 15th century doorway and a 16th century window. The south porch could be of almost any post-Reformation date. The font of 1441 has an inscription on the pedestal. The fragmentary sculpture of a Virgin and Child is late 13th century.

SHEVIOCK

St Peter and St Paul   SX 370550

The thin 13th century west tower has lancets and a broach-spire. The 14th century south transept has windows with a five pointed star in a circle as the main motif. Another window of this period from the former north transept has been transferred to the west end of an aisle added in the 15th century with windows and a wagon roof of that period and an arcade of six bays with piers of the Cornish standard type. The chancel is 14th century and has an image niche on the north jamb of the east window. In the south transept are effigies on tomb chests thought to be Sir Hugh Courtenay and his son Edward, d1370, and the latter's wife, these being placed in recesses in the end wall. There is a plain circular 13th century font. The bench ends have tracery and Renaissance motifs.

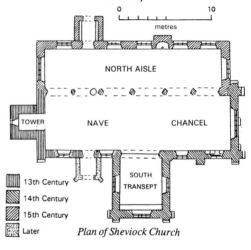

Plan of Sheviock Church

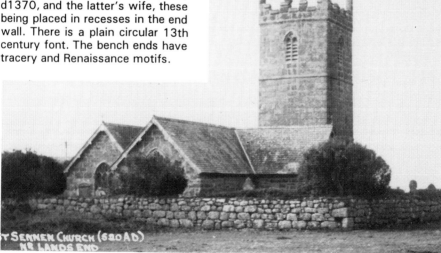

Sennen Church

SITHNEY   *St Siddinius*   SW 636290

The north end of a 12th or 13th century north transept survives beyond the north aisle and there is also early masonry in the chancel. The narrow south transept is perhaps 16th century but the nave and aisles, the porch and tower are late 14th to 15th century. There are arcades of six bays with Cornish standard piers, those on the north having horizontal leaves on the capitals. The arches between the chancel and north chapel are lower than the rest. The unbuttressed tower of granite blocks has three lofty stages and pinnacles. The church contains a small round Norman font and a 13th century cross-slab. The pillar on a pedestal to John Oliver in the churchyard was erected by his son in 1741.

SOUTH HILL   *St Sampson*   SX 329726

Most of the church consecrated in 1333 still remains, the only later medieval parts being the upper part of the tower of large granite blocks and the south aisle with a typical Cornish arcade and a fine wagon roof, plus the porch. The tower parapet is supported by twelve apostles. The aisle has replaced the south transept of a cruciform church with angle buttresses on all the parts. A window in the chancel south wall adjoins still older sedilia, i.e. 13th century, but the piscina with ogees and crockets is clearly of c1330. A squint from the north transept opens into the western of two ogival-headed tomb recesses. The east window has typical Decorated style tracery with pointed trefoils and quatrefoils and dagger-shaped lights. The Norman font has corner faces, trees of life and long animals. There is an incised slab to John Manaton, d1507, and his wife. In the churchyard is a 6th or 7th century inscribed stone with an XP monogram and the inscription "Cumregni Fili Mauci".

Sithney Church

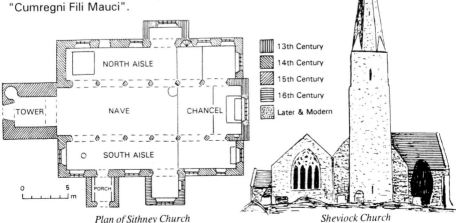

▦	13th Century
▨	14th Century
▧	15th Century
▤	16th Century
▦	Later & Modern

Plan of Sithney Church

Sheviock Church

Tower at Stratton

South Petherwin Church

SOUTH PETHERWIN   *St Paternus*   SX 309819

Relics of a Norman church are the north doorway with one order of colonettes and a crenellation motif on the voussoirs, a nearby stoup, and the large capital from a former arcade, the west respond of which was revealed in 1889. The circular font with octagonal supports and flat pointed arches is 13th century. The north arcade with moulded capitals on square piers with demi-shafts and double-chamfered arches is 14th century. The two lower arches between the chancel and north chapel are 15th century, as are the other features such as the low three-stage tower with set-back buttresses, the three east windows of four lights, and the north and south porches with wagon roofs. One south window has fragments of old glass. Parts of the rood screen are now made into a tower screen. The pulpit has linenfold panels but is dated 1631. There are Royal Arms of James I and parts of pews of the same period appear in the reading desk.

STITHIANS   *St Stedyana*   SW 731371

The 14th century north aisle has buttresses, renewed windows with Geometrical tracery and a six-bay arcade of standard Cornish type. The south aisle is clearly later, having an arcade with flatter arches on square piers with four attached shafts. The tower has three stages with set-back buttresses and panelled pinnacles, and the arch towards the nave has attached shafts. The piscina sits on a Norman corbel with animals facing each other. The plain pulpit is Georgian. In the churchyard is an early cross with a Crucifixion scene.

STOKE CLIMSLAND   *Dedication Unknown*   SX 361744

The east responds of the six bay arcades are the only relics of the church dedicated in 1321. The arcades have square piers with four attached shafts with double chamfered arches. The lower arches flanking the chancel are later. The west tower of three stages with granite blocks has set-back buttresses. The wagon roofs are original late medieval work but the windows are all restored. On the south side is the rood-loft staircase. A 17th century slate to John Bagwill has a figure of Death on it.

STRATTON   *St Andrew*   SX 232065

The effigy of a cross-legged knight set on the sill of a north window may be Sir Ranulph de Blanchminster. In his will of 1348 he asked to be buried in the north aisle then under construction. The three west bays of this remain, with square piers with attached shafts and double-chamfered pointed arches. The south arcade is of the Cornish standard late medieval type and there are original wagon roofs. Of the 16th century are the Easter Sepulchre in the chancel and the west tower with set-back buttresses with the ends pointed. There is a plain circular Norman font. In the nave are old bench ends. The porch contains the door from a former prison. There is a Jacobean font and there are Royal Arms with strapwork decoration. Set on a slate are brasses of Sir John Arundell of Trerice, d1561 and two wives.

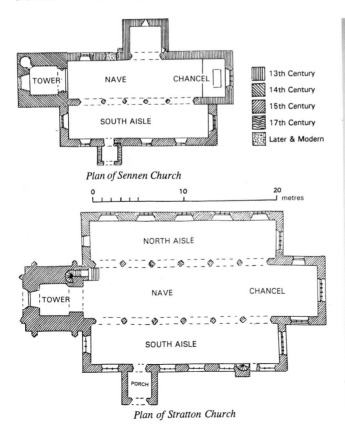

Plan of Sennen Church

Plan of Stratton Church

Stoke Climsland Church

TALLAND   *St Tallanus*   SX 228516

A detached tower south of the church is now connected to it by a late medieval porch with an original wagon roof. The lower stage of the tower may be as old as the 13th century west and east ends of the church. The west end has three lancets, the central one set over a broad buttress. Two other buttresses flank it. The south aisle with a granite six bay arcade of Cornish standard type and a fine wagon roof is late medieval, and the north transept also appears to be all of that period. The transept contains Jacobean seats, and the pulpit is Jacobean. The choir stalls contain material from the pew of the Beville family. There are bench ends of the 1520s and c1600. The tomb chest and recumbent figure of John Beville, d1578, were made by Peter Crocker. There is a slate plate to Joanna Mellow, d1625, depicted with a baby.

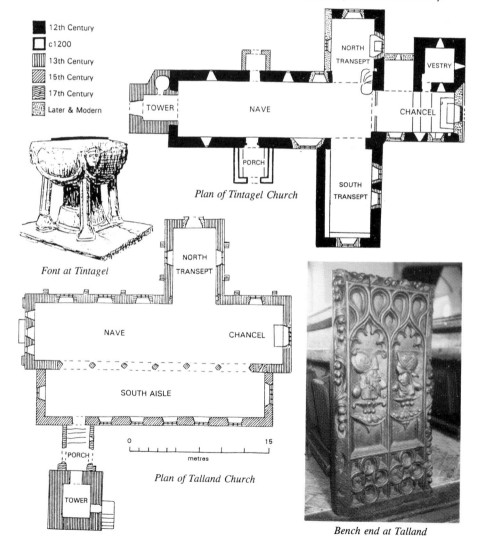

12th Century
c1200
13th Century
15th Century
17th Century
Later & Modern

Plan of Tintagel Church

Font at Tintagel

Plan of Talland Church

Bench end at Talland

Tintagel Church

Talland Church

TIDEFORD   *St Luke*   SX 347596

In the church of 1845 designed by Wightwick is a Norman font with corner faces and large rosettes. It once lay in the chapel of St Luke near Bolventor on Bodmin Moor.

TINTAGEL   *St Merteriana*   SX 050885

The church lies alone west of the village. It is Norman and lacks the later medieval additions usual in Cornwall. Only the tower top is of that period, the lower stage probably being 13th century. At that level the otherwise polygonal stair turret on the NE is square. A 13th century arch and 15th century screen divide off a long nave from a narrower chancel. Both have Norman windows and the nave has original north and south doorways, the former having original ironwork on the door and the latter having one order of columns with scalloped capitals and being reached through a porch probably of c1200. One chancel north window now looks into the chapel of St Symphorian, also Norman with original north and east windows. There are no proper arches between the nave and transepts. Both are Norman but the north transept has a 13th century triple lancet east window, a later north window and a rebuilt west wall, whilst the south transept has a pair of 13th century east windows with pairs of cusped lancets. This transept has been lengthened and has a stone bench against the whole of the west and south walls. The font has corner faces and five supports, those at the corners being octagonal. The reredos is made up from old bench ends. There is a 13th century slab with a head over a foliated cross. The brass half effigy of Joan Kelly is of c1430. In the church is a Roman milestone with an iscription referring to the Emperor Licinius (reigned 308-24).

Talland Church

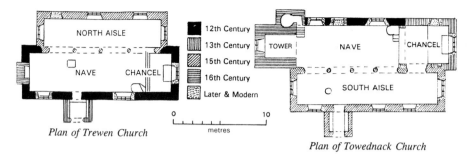

■	12th Century
▥	13th Century
▨	15th Century
▤	16th Century
▦	Later & Modern

0 _____ 10
metres

Plan of Trewen Church

Plan of Towednack Church

TOWEDNACK   *St Tewennochus*   SW 487387

The church ranked only as a chapel-of-ease until 1902. The nave north wall is 12th or 13th century, although the blocked doorway is later medieval and the windows are Victorian. A new chancel with a double-chamfered chancel arch was added c1300. There is renewed intersecting tracery in the east window and there is an altar slab with consecration crosses. The south aisle with a porch and four narrow four-centred arches on granite piers to the nave, and a further arch for the south chapel, is 15th century. The west tower with a NE stair turret is 16th century. The granite font with corner faces is dated 1720 and is set on the inverted bowl of a Norman font. In the porch is a stone with an incised cross.

TREGONY   *St Cuby*   SW 928453

The diagonally buttressed west tower with a NE stair turret is 14th century. The nave, south aisle and north transept retain no old features but there is a Norman font. The vaulted porch with cross-ribs has carved heads and interesting capitals on the outer entrance. There are Royal Arms of James II dated 1685.

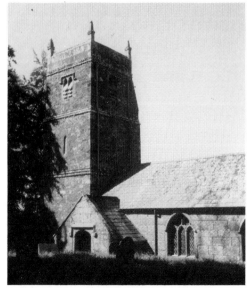

Treneglos Church

Tregony Church

TREMAINE   *St Winwallo*   SX 235890

This is a small single chamber on a hill. The north doorway with a mutilated tympanum is Norman. The east wall and the south wall east of the 17th century porch are 15th century. The tower is also of that date. It has Victorian buttresses on the south and north sides. The stair cut into the north wall inner face led to the former rood loft. The Norman font has a cable moulding.

TRENEGLOS   *St Gregory*   SX 235890

The church was rebuilt in 1858 but the tower seems medieval. Other old features are the small circular font with corner faces, the wagon roof in the porch, and the Norman tympanum with a tree set between two lions.

TRESILLIAN   *Dedication Unknown*   SW 870465

The church was rebuilt in 1878 by Edmund Sedding but contains a font from Merther with corner projections.

TRESLOTHAN   *St John*   SW 650378

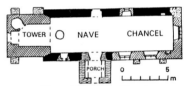

Plan of Tremaine Church

A 15th century granite font with angels with shields from Camborne and a late medieval alabaster panel lie in a chapel rebuilt in 1841 by Wightwick which originally served Pendarves House, demolished in 1955. The family mausoleum lies nearby.

TRESMEER   *St Nicholas*   SX 234875

The drastic restoration of 1880 has left a few 13th century triple lancets, a circular font with a cable moulding near the top and an unbuttressed 15th century tower.

TREVALGA   *St Petrock*   SX 081900

The church lacks the late medieval additions common in Cornwall. The small two-light windows of the north transept suggest a 13th century date, and the plain tower may also be of that period. A squint connects the transept and the chancel, both of which have old roofs. The reredos is a carved 16th century Flemish triptych.

TREWEN   *St Michael*   SX 252836

This is a small church with a north aisle with straight headed windows and an arcade of five low bays of the usual Cornish type. Inside is a plain square Norman font.

Trevalga Church

TROON   *St Ia*   SW 658382

The lower parts survive of a rectangular chapel with north and south doorways. The west end overlies the remains of a massive drystone baptistry of early date.

TRURO   *St Mary*   SW 826449

Beyond the south aisle of the choir of the cathedral built between 1880 and 1910 to a design by John L.Pearson, and connected to it by a narrow outer aisle, is the south aisle of the former parish church of St Mary. The aisle is a superb piece of work dating from 1504-18, probably by the same masons as the Probus tower since it shares the motif of two layers of decoration on the plinth. The aisle is of six bays with four-light windows with the centre mullion more substantial than those on either side. There is blank tracery in the window spandrels and there are quatrefoils on the battlements. Parts of the roof and some of the glass are also old. The church originally had a tower with a spire 38m high which was rebuilt in 1768. In the crypt are several 18th and 19th century monuments to the Vyvyan family and a monument with reclining effigies of Richard Robarts, d1614, and his wife. The architecture and furnishings of the rest of the cathedral lie beyond the scope of this book.

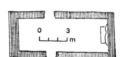

St Ia's Chapel, Troon: plan

Tywardreath Church

Aisle of St Mary's, now part of Truro Cathedral

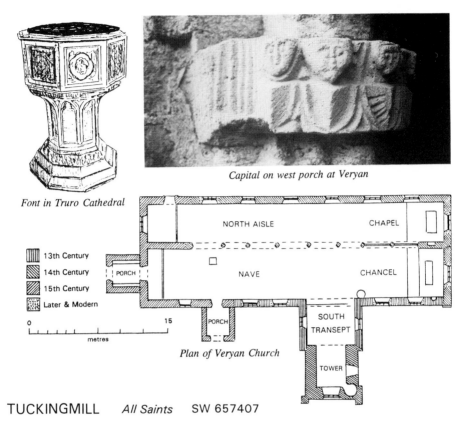

Capital on west porch at Veryan

Font in Truro Cathedral

Plan of Veryan Church

13th Century
14th Century
15th Century
Later & Modern

0   15
metres

NORTH AISLE   CHAPEL

PORCH

NAVE   CHANCEL

PORCH

SOUTH TRANSEPT

TOWER

TUCKINGMILL   *All Saints*   SW 657407

Inside the neo-Norman church of 1843-4 designed by J. Hayward lies a font of c1100 from St Derwa's Chapel, Mendarva.

TYWARDREATH   *St Andrew*   SX 085543

Little survived the rebuilding of 1880 by Robert Coad apart from the 14th century west tower of four stages with a SE stair turret, and the 15th century octagonal font with shields in quatrefoils. The pulpit is made up of old bench ends. The earliest monuments are the foliated cross slab to Thomas Colyns, d1534, prior of Tywardreath Priory, a slate plate to a lady, 1636, and a relief of Jane Pole, d1795.

VERYAN   *St Symphonian*   SW 916396

This is quite a long church, the arcade of standard Cornish type being of eight bays with limestone capitals with leaves on the abaci set upon granite piers. Solid wall takes the place of the possible ninth bay at the west end. The church has porches to the south and west since the slate 14th century tower with clasping angle buttresses lies south of a south transept with Y-tracery in its windows. The west porch doorway has unusual capitals with rows of heads. The font looks Norman but may actually be later medieval. Genuine Norman are the heads from a corbel table in and upon the porch. Parts of the rood screen survive.

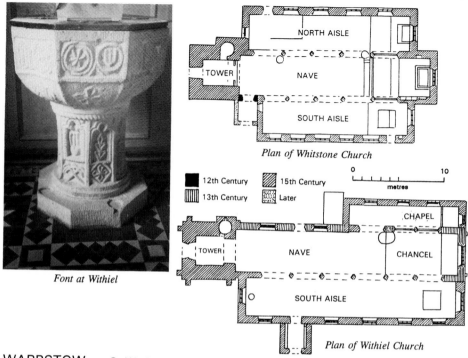

NORTH AISLE

TOWER   NAVE

SOUTH AISLE

Plan of Whitstone Church

■ 12th Century ▨ 15th Century
▥ 13th Century ▦ Later

0   10
metres

.CHAPEL

TOWER   NAVE   CHANCEL

SOUTH AISLE

Plan of Withiel Church

Font at Withiel

WARBSTOW   *St Werburgh*   SX 205904

The church is late medieval with a plain two-stage west tower and a low granite north arcade with four-centred arches of typical Cornish type. The Norman font has faces at the corners and stylized six-petalled flowers in niches on the sides.

WARLEGGAN   *St Bartholomew*   SX 156691

The unbuttressed west tower of two stages had a spire until it collapsed in 1818. A 13th century lancet remains on the north side of the church, whilst the south side has a 15th century aisle with granite piers of the usual type. The only ancient feature inside is the Royal Arms of 1664 with strapwork.

WASHAWAY   *St Conan*   SX 035700

In the church of 1882 lies an 11th century font with interlacing and animals from Lanteglos-by-Camelford.

WEEK ST MARY   *Nativity of St Mary*   SX 237977

The south arcade with piers of polyphant stone is late 14th century. The east bays and the north arcade of granite are later. Most of the windows are restored but some old work remains in the wagon roofs. The unbuttressed west tower of three stages has carved figures on the plinth and castellated pinnacles. In a farmhouse nearby are parts of the buildings of the college of priests founded by Thomasine Bonaventure in the early 16th century.

WENDRON   *St Wendron*   SW 678311

One 13th century cusped lancet remains in the chancel north wall, which also contains a tomb recess. The north aisle and north transept are 14th century. A squint connects the chancel and transepts. The 15th century south aisle has a porch with set-back buttresses. The arcade of standard Cornish type has five arches towards the nave and two narrower arches (perhaps for tombs) with a still lower one between them towards the chancel. The west tower has a diagonal NW corner buttress with a stair turret adjoining. The font with quatrefoils and corner shafts is 14th century. The brass to Rector William Penhalluryk, d1535, is headless. There is a 16th century tablet in the chancel. By the porch is a Celtic cross head and there is a slab with an incised cross with the head encircled. The lychgate upper room is 17th century.

WERRINGTON   *St Martin*   SX 328876

In 1742 the church was entirely rebuilt except for the west tower with diagonal buttresses and pinnacles to which was added a castellated screen wall with corner turrets and black quatrefoils plus statues in niches. The interior has been remodelled and the only items of interest within are a Norman font with heads on the corners of the base and a monument with kneeling figures of the Drake family.

WHITSTONE   *St Anne*   SX 264986

The church lies south of the village and is mostly late medieval with arcades of five bays of the usual Cornish type and an unbuttressed west tower with a NE stair turret, but there was a heavy restoration by Hooper in 1882. The plain south doorway is Norman and so is the circular font with an undulating leaf-frieze. The porch lies west of the south aisle and there is a window with an original grille between them. Hidden amongst the old roof beams in the north aisle is a green man (only visible from the west). On the outside of the south wall is a slate slab to Thomas Edgcumbe, d1712. A holy well lies built into the slope SE of the church.

Warbstow Church

Withiel Church

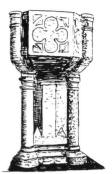

Font at Zennor

WITHIEL   *St Clement*   SW 994654

The north doorway suggests a 13th century date for the nave and the chancel is probably also of that date. To them have been added a granite south aisle with a porch and a north chapel, both with arcades of the usual Cornish late medieval type. The font is also late medieval and there are original wagon-roofs.

ZENNOR   *St Senner*   SW 455385

The nave south wall is Norman, with one renewed small window. The south transept has walls with a battered base. It and the chancel are probably 13th century and are connected by a later squint. The transept has a renewed south window of c1300. The octagonal font on five supports with the outer ones corbelling out like stove-pipes and quatrefoils on the bowl is also probably of about that period. The unbuttressed west tower is late 14th or 15th century and the wide north aisle with a six bay arcade of double-chamfered arches on octagonal piers is 15th century. The aisle west window is 16th century. A seat in the chancel has been made from two former bench ends, one of which is carved with a mermaid. The head of an ancient cross lies by the churchyard entrance.

Interior of Zennor Church

OTHER ANGLICAN CHURCHES IN CORNWALL

BALDHU - St Michael - c1848 by William White.
BUDE - St Michael - 1835 by Wightwick, but enlarged in 1876.
CAMELFORD - St Thomas - By Sir Charles Nicholson, consecrated 1938.
CHACEWATER - St Paul - Tower 1828, rest of 1892 by Edmund Sedding.
CHARLESTOWN - St Paul - 1849 by Eales.
DELABOLE - St John - c1880 by Hine and Odgers.
DEVORAN - St John - 1855-6 by J.L.Pearson. Aisleless, with a polygonal chancel.
FALMOUTH - All Saints - 1887-90 by J.D.Sedding. Five lancets at the west end.
FLUSHING - St Peter - 1842.
GODOLPHIN - St John the Baptist - 1849-59 by J.P.St Aubyn.
GRAMPOUND - St Nunn - 15th century chapel entirely rebuilt in 1869.
HAYLE - St Elwyn - 1886-8 by J.D.Sedding. Aisle with apsed east end.
HESSENFORD - St Anne - 1832, but rebuilt in 1871 to a design by J.P.St Aubyn.
MARAZION - All Saints - 1861 by J.P.St Aubyn.
MITHIAN - St Peter - 1861 by William White. Cruciform. Tower rebuilt in 1928.
NEWLYN - St Peter - Rebuilt by Perrow in 1865. Aisle & transept added 1881-6.
NEWQUAY - St Michael - 1909-11 by Sebastian Comper. Large, Cornish medieval.
PENDEEN - St John - 1851, designed by the parson and built by his villagers.
PENPONDS - Holy Trinity - 1854 by J.P.St Aubyn
PENZANCE - St Mary - 1832-5 by Charles Hutchins. Engaged west tower. East apse.
PENZANCE - St Paul - 1843, enlarged by J.W.Trounson in 1893. Clarence Street.
PORTREATH - St Mary - 1841 by Wightwick. Pointed windows and a bellcote.
ST DAY - Holy Trinity - 1828 by Charles Hutchins. Commissioners' type church.
TEMPLE - St Catherine - Rebuilt 1883 by S.Trevail. Plain Norman font inside.
TORPOINT - St James - 1819 with chancel added 1885. Lancets.
TREVENSON - Chapel of ease to Illogan built in 1806-9. Thin castellated tower.
TREVERBYN - 1848-50 by G.E.Street. Only his second church, first was at Par.
TRURO - St Paul - 1848 with chancel added by J.D.Sedding in 1882-4.
PENTEWAN, PORTHPEAN, & PORT ISAAC have undated 19th century churches.

MANORIAL CHAPELS

BODINNICK - Latterly a boat-shed. Fine north
  doorway with scrolled ends to the label. Tiny
  embattled turret rising out of the roof.
CAPE CORNWALL - Small, now a farm building.
MILLBROOK - Remnant of Inswork manor house.
SHILLINGHAM - Medieval chapel ruin adjoins house.
TINTEN - 15th century east window. Now a barn.
TRECARREL - Late medieval, built by Henry Trecarrel.

St Mary's, Isles of Scilly:

ISLES OF SCILLY CHURCHES

BRYHER, All Saints - Built 1742, rebuilt in 1822.
ST HELEN'S - Very ruined. Had nave, chancel, north
  aisle. 6th century hut cells surround the site.
ST MARY'S - East end and transepts demolished after
  Hugh Town church built in 1838. Nave has reset
  Norman doorway to former porch, two mullioned
  windows, modern NW doorway.
ST MARTIN'S is of 1867, ST AGNES is of c1845.
ST NICHOLAS on TRESCO dates from 1877-9.

12th Century
17th Century
Later & Modern

St Mary's, Isles of Scilly

GLOSSARY OF ARCHITECTURAL TERMS

Abacus	- A flat slab on top of a capital.
Apse	- Semi-circular or polygonal east end of a church containing an altar.
Ashlar	- Masonry of blocks with even faces and square edges.
Baroque	- A whimsical and odd form of the Classical architectural style.
Beakhead	- Decorative motif of bird or beast heads, often biting a roll moulding.
Broaches	- Sloping half pyramids adapting an octagonal spire to a square tower.
Cartouche	- A tablet with an ornate frame, usually enclosing an inscription.
Chancel	- The eastern part of a church used by the clergy.
Chevron Ornament	- A Norman ornament with continuous Vs forming a zig-zag.
Clerestory	- An upper storey pierced by windows lighting the floor below.
Collar Beam	- A tie-beam used higher up near the apex of the roof.
Corbel Table	- A row of corbels supporting the eaves of a roof.
Crossing Tower	- A tower built on four arches in the middle of a cruciform church.
Cruciform Church	- A cross-shaped church with transepts forming the arms of the cross.
Cusp	- A projecting point between the foils of a foiled Gothic arch.
Dado	- The decorative covering of the lower part of a wall or screen.
Decorated	- The architecture style in vogue in England c1300-1380.
Dog Tooth	- Four pointed stars placed diagonally and raised pyramidally.
Easter Sepulchre	- A recess in a chancel which received an effigy of Christ at Easter.
Elizabethan	- Of the time of Queen Elizabeth I (1558-1603).
Fan Vault	- Vault with fan-like patterns. In fashion from c1440 to 1530.
Flamboyant	- The latest phase of French Gothic with indulating window tracery.
Fleuron	- A decorative carved flower or leaf.
Foil	- A lobe formed by the cusping of a circle or arch.
Four Centred Arch	- A low, flattish arch with each curve drawn from two compass points.
Head Stops	- Heads of humans or beasts forming the ends of a hoodmould.
Hoodmould	- A projecting moulding above a lintel or arch to throw off water.
Jacobean	- Of the time of King James I (1603-25).
Jamb	- The side of a doorway, window, or other opening.
Lancet	- A long and comparatively narrow window with a pointed head.
Light	- A compartment of a window.
Lintel	- A horizontal stone or beam spanning an opening.
Miserichord	- Bracket underneath hinged choir stall seat to support standing person.
Mullion	- A vertical member dividing the lights of a window.
Nave	- The part of a church in which the congregation sits or stands.
Norman	- A division of English Romanesque architecture from 1066 to 1200.
Ogival Arch	- Arch of oriental origin with both convex and concave curves.
Pediment	- Low-pitch gable used in classical and neo-classical architecture.
Perpendicular	- The architectural style in vogue in England c1380-1540.
Pilaster	- Flat buttress or pier attached to a wall.
Piscina	- A stone basin used for rinsing out holy vessels after a mass.
Plinth	- The projecting base of a wall.
Quoins	- Dressed stones at the corners of a building.
Rere-Arch	- An arch on the inside face of a window embrasure or doorway.
Reredos	- Structure behind and above an altar forming a backdrop to it.
Respond	- A half pier or column bonded into a wall and carrying an arch.
Reticulation	- Tracery with a net-like appearence. Current c1330-70.
Rood Screen	- A screen with a crucifix mounted on it between a nave and chancel.
Sedilia	- Seats for clergy (usually three) in the south wall of a chancel.
Spandrel	- The surface between two arches or between an arch and a corner.
Squint	- Opening allowing the main altar to be seen from a subsiderary one.
Tester	- A sounding board above a 17th or 18th century pulpit.
Tie-Beam	- A beam connecting the slopes of a roof at or near its foot.
Tracery	- Intersecting ribwork in the upper part of a later Gothic window.
Transom	- A horizontal member dividing the lights of a window.
Tympanum	- The space between the lintel of a doorway and the arch above it.
Venetian Window	- Window with square headed light on either side of an arched light.
Victorian	- Of the time of Queen Victoria (1837-1901).
Voussoir	- A wedge shaped stone forming part of an arch.